THE MOMENT OF TRUTH

Other works by the same author

God is with Us
In Time of Temptation
Meeting God in Man
Pain and Providence
Living in Hope
We are Future
Hidden God
Meditations
Open Spirit

THE MOMENT OF TRUTH

Mysterium Mortis

by

LADISLAUS BOROS

LONDON
SEARCH PRESS

SEARCH PRESS LIMITED
85 Gloucester Road, London SW7 4SU

First Publication in Great Britain 1965
Paperback edition May 1969
Second impression September 1969
Third impression 1972
Fourth impression 1973

Translated by Gregory Bainbridge

ISBN: 0 85532 042 7

PRINTED IN GREAT BRITAIN BY
REDWOOD BURN LIMITED, TROWBRIDGE & ESHER

SET IN 'MONOTYPE' BELL

NIHIL OBSTAT: ANDREAS J. MOORE, CENSOR DEPUTATUS; IMPRIMATUR:
PATRITIUS CASEY, VIC. GEN., WESTMONASTERII, DIE 2 APRILIS 1965.

CONTENTS

INTRODUCTION

" 'You know what they say: "It takes nine months to create a man, and only a single day to destroy him." We both of us have known the truth of this as well as any one could ever know it. . . . Listen, May: it does not take nine months to make a man, it takes fifty years—fifty years of sacrifice, of determination, of—so many things! And when that man has been achieved, when there is no childishness left in him, nor any adolescence, when he is truly, utterly, a man—the only thing he is good for is to die.' "

This bitter remark, taken from the last page of André Malraux's *Man's Estate*,[1]* was intended by the author of the novel to be an expression of the futility of life. For, if human death has no meaning, then the whole of life is nothing but emptiness. If, on the other hand, there is in death a fullness of being which life does not possess, then life itself must be subjected to a thoroughgoing re-interpretation and revaluation. It is a strange thing that the search for some content in life and some continuity in human existence should have to start off as an enquiry into the meaning of death!

It is not easy for us to do this nowadays. The violent, primitive process of death is becoming so obscured by our general forgetfulness of the meaning of all natural processes that we are no longer disturbed by it. There

* The notes will be found grouped at the end of the work.

are few happenings to which we have grown so blind as we are to death. But to be forgetful of death is to be forgetful of life, whereas thinking of one's death is an act in which life begins once more to appear as a source of light. A man who knows death, also knows life. The converse is true, too: the man who is forgetful of death, is forgetful of life also.

When considered from a biological and medical point of view, death is apprehended in that aspect of its being that is accessible to experimental science, that is, as a dissolution, an occurrence to be endured, a deprivation of consciousness, a destruction. Metaphysical anthropology, on the other hand, asks the question whether this complete removal from self which we undergo in death does not conceal a much more fundamental process which could be described, not in terms of a dissolution and an endurance of suffering, but rather in terms of the progressive achievement of selfhood, of actively initiating the self to life. As an approach to a consideration of this metaphysical problem, let me give, in outline, a picture of death as I see it—a picture the accuracy of which I propose to establish in the course of the following investigation. But first of all a brief sketch, without going into more precise detail.

In death the individual existence takes its place on the confines of all being, suddenly awake, in full knowledge and liberty. The hidden dynamism of existence by which a man has lived until then—though without his ever having been able to exploit it in its fullest measure—is now brought to completion, freely and consciously. Man's deepest being comes rushing towards him. With it comes all at once and all together the universe he has always borne hidden within himself, the universe with which he was already most intimately united, and which, in one way or other, was always being produced from within him. Humanity too, everywhere driven by a like force, a humanity that bears within itself, all unsuspecting, a splendour he could never have imagined, also comes rushing towards him. Being flows towards him like a boundless stream of things, meanings, persons and happenings, ready to convey him right into the Godhead. Yes; God himself stretches out his hand for him; God who, in every stirring of his existence, had been in him as his deepest mystery, from the stuff of which he had always been forming himself; God who had ever been driving him on towards an eternal destiny. There now man stands, free to accept or reject this splendour. In a last, final decision he either allows this flood of realities to flow past him, while he stands there eternally turned to stone, like a rock past which the life-giving stream flows on, noble enough in himself no doubt, but abandoned and eternally alone; or he allows himself to be carried along by this flood, becomes part of it and flows on into eternal fulfilment.

This is the meaning of the hypothesis which we shall try to justify in two successive essays, the first philosophical, the second theological. It may be stated thus: *Death gives man the opportunity of posing his first completely personal act; death is, therefore, by reason of its very being, the moment above all others for the awakening of consciousness, for freedom, for the encounter with God, for the final decision about his eternal destiny.* This way of viewing the subject transforms the expression of futility we quoted at the beginning into an exhortation to confidence. In the course of the following discussion this idea will—rather in the form of a dissertation (for which we ask the reader's indulgence)—be described as the "hypothesis of a final decision".

In its original form—the structure of which has for the most part been retained—the following essay was written in quite a short time and composed *currente calamo* without a break.[2] Since I want to avoid anything that might disturb the unity of treatment of this problem as a whole, I have thought it advisable to clear the ground by discussing at the outset all the methodological points necessary for the understanding of the whole work.

I

THE METHODOLOGICAL POSTULATES FOR AN ANALYSIS OF DEATH

I

THE METHODOLOGICAL POSTULATES FOR AN ANALYSIS OF DEATH

1. *Death as a Metaphysical Process*

ANY ATTEMPT to clarify the various questions connected with human death brings the philosopher up against a series of methodological difficulties—and this present one is perhaps, for the moment, going to tax the reader's patience! Let me at once state the most important and fundamental of these difficulties: no man has a *direct experience* of death. What we go through as we watch at someone's death-bed is assuredly not death in its inner reality; it is only the outward aspect of death. We cannot expect to receive a decisive, revealing answer from people who have been near death, or have been given up for dead by those about them. The philosopher will get no assistance from those who are professionally concerned with the dying. Though it is true that many of them have gained deep insights into the death-struggle, none ever saw the actual passing-over. This statement requires further explanation.

Death cannot be gone through from outside, reproduced, as it were, *in vitro*. Each one of us must accept it absolutely alone, must and can meet death only once. The outsider, for example a doctor, can assist the dying person, can accompany him on the way of his agony, but cannot enter with him into his actual death. The doctor and the philosopher mean different processes when they speak of death. For this reason the philosophical investigation we are undertaking requires us to direct our thinking along radically different lines from those followed by doctors. The doctor observes how in the dying man the flame of life burns slowly lower and lower, growing feebler every moment until it is hardly perceptible. With the help of powerful drugs or other exceptional means the doctor can still revive the sinking flame of life, but the physiological spontaneity of life continues to get weaker and weaker. The essential bodily functions come to a stop. The body begins to decompose, and when that happens, the most elementary co-ordination of the various individual functions is ended. Particular tissues or whole organs can indeed be preserved intact artificially, but life as a whole has become impossible; the person has "died". But does that mean that he is "dead"? The question points to a *distinction between dying and death* which is of fundamental importance to our analysis.

Medical science studies those aspects of life that Aristotle calls "physics": that is, things that are palpable, observable, experimentally demonstrable. But underlying this is the whole complex of what lies beyond, of "metaphysics". When a philosopher speaks of death he is speaking of a *metaphysical process*, which he generally describes as the "separation of the soul from the body".[3] Except in cases of instantaneous destruction of the whole organism this separation does not apparently coincide with the cessation of the vital functions. Recent experiments in resuscitation show that life "withdraws" very slowly and can remain for a long time in a body that to all appearances has become "incapable of living". Intra-arterial and intracardiac injections (adrenalin and atropin) combined with an artificial supply of oxygen and —where necessary—heart-massage, can set some kind of life on its spasmodic course again, even if only for a short time in most cases. There comes a moment, however, when all these efforts fail. This indicates that the "separation of the soul from the body" has possibly already taken place. This metaphysical moment, which it is not possible to determine by simple observation, is what we call "death". The hypothesis of a final decision is concerned exclusively with the "moment of death" as understood in this sense.

Stated thus, the question of death is one of urgent theological significance. Philosophical reflexions on death in the thirties brought about a great change in theological perspectives.[4] Until then the interest of theologians (if we leave out of account their discussions of the preliminaries to death, the condition of man *before death*) was concentrated on an evaluation of the conditions of the soul separated from the body *after death*. The classic answers are well known: with the separation of the soul from the body man's pilgrimage comes to a definite end; immediately after the particular judgement the soul passes into one of three—or, if we include limbo, which so many adopt as a theological hypothesis, of four —"places for departed souls", heaven, hell or purgatory, where it awaits the final resurrection at the end of time. The great turning point in theological reflexion came when death itself began to be examined by the theologians.[5] What really happens to the whole man *at the moment of death*?

The final decision which we have assumed as an hypothesis occurs neither before nor after death, but *in* death. But immediately the objection will be raised: "Surely you cannot assume that anyone really makes the first completely personal act of his life when he is in the state of bodily and spiritual torment we call the throes of death, or, it may be, the state of insensibility no less proper to the process of dying?" From what has been said, it is clear that this objection is like forcing an already open door. Bringing the final decision forward into the agony, into the state *before* death, would, indeed, betoken great naïveté of thought. It would deprive our arguments of all their power of conviction. On the other hand, the final decision does not take place *after* death either. Apart from the fact that such an assumption misconceives the metaphysical constitution of the completely personal act, it would also be contrary to the Church's teaching on the inalterability of the state a man reaches through his death.

2. *A Temporal Process in a Non-Temporal Transition*

Our task is to state as clearly as possible the meaning of the expression: "the moment of death". Accordingly we shall examine two further objections which attack precisely this point.

Firstly: "For the taking of a decision a certain interval of time is required. But, between 'before death' and 'after death' there is no intervening space of time. The transition must be thought of as a break that has nothing to do with time. But if death is something instantaneous and indivisible, it affords no possibility for a decision, for a decision is always an act extended over a period of time."[6] This argument is verbally very seductive, but logically it is open to question. It must of course be admitted that death as an instantaneous transformation can only occur in a non-temporal transition, and that death is thus not one moment in a temporal succession, but, as it were, a mere line of demarcation between two moments without any temporal extension of its own. But this only means that the last moment before the break and the first after it merge into one another. A line of demarcation without extension of its own does not, in metaphysical terms, bring about a separation within a succession conditioned by time and quantity. The moments of the soul's "separating" and "being separated" thus coincide. Therefore, the moment of death, the transition itself, is—when looked at from the subsequent condition—the last moment of the preceding condition, and—when viewed from the preceding condition—the first moment of the succeeding condition. So then, although the transition in death must be regarded as something non-temporal, i.e. outside time, the passing and what occurs in the passing are temporal. Because of this, the moment of death offers an opportunity for decision. If the transition in death was not non-temporal, the two moments of before and after could not merge into each other, bringing about a compound and—for that very reason—temporal reality. One suspects that there is another problem at the root of this first counter-argument, and we shall answer this at length when dealing with the next objection, since it gives us the possibility of formulating still more clearly the concept of the "moment of death".

Secondly: "The hypothesis of a final decision compresses a number of mental acts into one single moment: the act of completely personal decision; preceding this decision in time, an absolutely personal act of perception;

conditioning this perception, an awakening of the soul to its spirituality; and so forth. To be able to pose all these acts, the mind requires some length of time, however short. A single moment is not enough." This objection touches on the problem of temporality. To grasp this in its essentials is one of the hardest tasks in philosophy. Our answer is that the difficulty in question arises from a confusion between the different levels of temporality. The proof can be summarized as follows.

Our experience of time is founded on an observed movement of being. This occurs on different levels, according to the successive stages of being. The first stage in its totality may be called "the sub-personal time-level". At this level we observe a regular, uniform succession, splitting our world into innumerable flashes of existence, each one of which destroys our world and then re-creates it. Things emerge into being only for a moment and at once disappear into non-being. In other words, the world of our experience arises out of the hidden depths of being as successive moment succeeds to moment.

The second stage in the movement of being is that of our own inner, personal sense of time. At this level the successive moments no longer pass uniformly. Our personal duration takes on different forms: impetuous speed, gradual advance, indolent dawdling. His personal duration is something proper to each individual; it characterizes his mode of existence. Decisions of profound significance compress time and turn it into a kind of thick black line. Superficial decisions, on the other hand, register as mere specks in the course of our existence. We observe the difference in moments of existence when we compare our personal duration with the uniform movement of being on the sub-personal time-level.

Strictly speaking the progression of personal reality ought to be measured only by this reality itself. The practical necessities of social life compel us, however, to direct our individual (i.e. intensive) movement of being in accordance with a uniform and sub-personal (i.e. extensive) progression which is independent of us. Furthermore, the sub-personal movement of being is not fundamentally alien to our existence: we are deeply plunged into the sub-personal stream of being and are constantly carried along with it. This is why we are unable to realize our own total content of being, otherwise than in partial acts, in acts dissected into different incomplete functions. Our experience is a double one: on the one side, we have an inkling of what purely spiritual duration could be; on the other, we are unable to free ourselves from the segmented succession of a sub-personal movement of being.

It is different at the third stage, to which the soul belongs as it parts from the body and becomes fully awake to its own spirituality. In death the spiritual movement of being is liberated from the alien element of non-personal temporality. The spirit's succession now becomes entirely interior, that is, determined solely by the succession inherent in its exercise of its own being. This occurs in a total awareness and presence of being, and not in mere flashes that reach us only fragmentarily. Thus the spirit is no longer swept along by an alien succession. It is able to realize fully the whole continuity of its being, all at once, in one and the same act.

We cannot give complete expression to this spiritual process in our own concepts because these are formed on the second time-level. We speak of "partial realizations", of "single acts", each one of which must be actualized and de-actualized individually before a new act can be posed. We speak of the "continuous succession" of different functions, although we know that on the level of spiritual duration self-realization takes place in one single act, that is, in a total awareness and presence of being. Thus, although in death there is but one single act in the completely personal exercise of being, we can grasp the completeness of this single act only by describing it as a concentration of several spiritual acts, as if in death the spirit achieved its self-realization in separate acts, succeeding one another in time. This inexactitude of our language must be constantly borne in mind when we speak of the process of death; otherwise we make unnecessary difficulties for ourselves where, in fact, none exists.

3. *Death a Fundamental Modality of Living, Concrete Existence*

After this preliminary discussion of the concept "moment of death" we ask the crucial question: How can we make any statement at all about this moment? At the very beginning of this methodological introduction we referred to a difficulty that is inherent in the subject: philosophical reflexions on death seem to have no point since we have no direct experience of death. Modern philosophy has gone far towards answering this question. Martin Heidegger, in his book *Being and Time*, expressed himself very clearly on this point.[7] According to him, death is *a fundamental modality of living, concrete existence*. Our existence carries death within itself, and not only—or, at least, not primarily—because we can in reality die at any moment. Any given existence may be defined as a dedication to, an immersion in death, not only because it is on its way to meet death, but more truly essentially because it constantly realizes in itself the "situation" of death. This presence of death is so fundamental to existence that not one of its stirrings can be understood otherwise than in the light of a constitutive ordering towards death. In every act of existence death is present from the beginning. Its own end belongs of right to every existent being as an outstanding debt, a *perfectio debita*. The expression indicates something that is proper to a being, but which it does not yet possess. For example, an unripe fruit develops towards ripeness; it, and no other, brings itself to ripeness, and this characterizes its existence as a fruit. This "not yet" is comprised in its own existence, and attains expression in "ripeness". True, the presence of death in human existence cannot be grasped from this example without some qualification. It is much more intensive, more truly essential, more pervasive. Heidegger himself supplements the comparison in important respects.[8]

These analyses of Heidegger's seem to hark back to Augustinian thought. In his portrayal of man Augustine certainly makes of "dedication to death" an intrinsic determining factor of human existence. Man is, in fact, dying as long as he exists. "As doctors, when they examine the state of a patient and recognize that death is at hand, pronounce: 'He is dying, he will not recover', so we must say from the moment a man is born: 'He will not recover'."[9] Perhaps this remark again could be understood in the sense of a continual "threat" to existence by death, but Augustine's real thought—and in it he expresses too the essence of Heidegger's thought—may be seen in a complementary remark: "If each one of us begins to die—that is, to be in death—from the moment when death—that is, the ebb of life—began to work in him, then we must say we are in death from the moment we began to be in this body."[10]

This is an important point to make. Death has been introduced into the structure of living, concrete existence, and a path leading to a philosophy of death has in principle been opened up. For, when the figure of death makes its appearance in living existence, the philosopher is able to lay hold of death itself at the place where the various pointers to death with which existence furnishes him, intersect. To use another image: the philosopher's task is to discern the presence of death in an existence while it is still alive, and put together the picture of death from the mosaic fragments of so many scattered experiences of death. But how are we to obtain these pointers to death? How can death be discerned in our existence?

4. *The Workings of the Death-Process Revealed by the Transcendental Method*

If death really is a fundamental modality of living, concrete existence, then, in any given existence, it must always and everywhere be present; but what is always and everywhere present is not perceived. We take as little notice of it as we do of the beating of our heart, or of the air we breathe. It is like an atmosphere enveloping the landscape of our existence, and we have become so accustomed to it that our eyes no longer see it. What is closest to us is often farthest away. That is why we are never consciously and explicitly aware of death as a basic cause of the movements that occur in our mental activity. Death is the unreflexive, uncoordinated factor in our existence, one of those primitive metaphysical data that precede immediate experience. Human existence is lived out on different levels. It builds up from within, from an inner nucleus which ever eludes our grasp. It is, however, possible for philosophy to isolate and lay bare this thing in us which is constantly rising to the surface but is never actually grasped. This can be done by the *transcendental method,* that is to say, by an investigation of the acts of consciousness in order to find out just what implications they convey.[11] In other words, the transcendental method is the way that discloses how, in our acts, there is always being effected at the same time an accompanying process of penetration into the sphere of what gives birth to them, something welling up out of the depths of our human being.

Some historical examples will show us how this method has been used. Plato directed his efforts to revealing the absolute contained in every experience. He had recognized intuitively that there is in us a primitive knowledge which is not obtained from experience, but precedes and conditions experience. He called these primitive data "ideas". Therefore, in working out his theory of ideas, Plato was actually using a philosophy based on the transcendental method. St Augustine dealt with the same basic problem. In every act of concrete existence he decried something transcendent that constantly eludes the grasp of our thought. He called this "the realm of eternal truths", and held that man unconsciously gains possession of it in every act of knowing, and that its presence, though realized only in an unconscious manner, floods the spirit with "light". His theory of "eternal truths" and "illumination", and hence his transcendental method, influenced both early and later Scholasticism. There is no doubt that the method is present in St Thomas Aquinas and that it played a decisive part in his teaching about the apriority of our knowledge. In the later developments of Scholasticism it was more and more concealed by a preponderance of Aristotelianism until it disappeared almost completely. Kant discovered it afresh and used it in his *Critique of Pure Reason* to re-establish the connexion between our empirical knowledge and its *a priori* foundations. In German idealist philosophy, in Fichte, Schelling and Hegel, the transcendental method attained a perfection which, until then, had not been thought possible. Vast areas of the activity of human consciousness were studied with its help, so as to reveal the *a priori* data which are contained in them, providing them with both a foundation and norms. In twentieth-century philosophy the transcendental method has been recognized as the appropriate instrument and process of metaphysical thought. Husserl's "reductions" and Heidegger's "expositions" bear witness to the effectiveness of this method. With Maréchal it provided a new foundation for metaphysics—in the immediate, it is true, for epistemology alone—and it has made a decisive contribution to the development of a completely new atmosphere in Scholastic thought. Perhaps the most important representative of the transcendental method is Blondel. His system is a veritable ordnance survey of the regions of the human person right up to their extreme limits, and a bringing to light (i.e. conscious perception) of what in its deepest reality the person had always been and willed. He has described his method as follows: "The method we must use . . . may be called a method of 'implication' and 'explicitation'. These expressions simply mean that, instead of running away, as it were, from the data of reality and from concrete thoughts, we have to bring to light what they envelop, what they, in the etymological meaning of the word, *suppose*; what makes them possible and gives them their consistency." "Implication means the discovery of what is, indeed, present but not adverted to, not yet expressly recognized or formulated."[12]

All these achievements of thought, as varied, even as contrary to one another as they may be, are related in one respect: the basis for all of them is the conviction that man, although he is in the world and, therefore, primarily not in his right place, at ease with himself, yet goes out to encounter the world from a spiritual depth that reaches further than any leadline can plumb. Into every act of his encounter with the world there enters, imperceptibly, an element from out of the unfathomable. In the view we are examining, man's fundamental metaphysical constitution lies in the fact that, while he draws his life from an incomparable abundance of spiritual wealth, he is yet condemned ever to deal with a superficial and fragmentary world. From this original experience, from the perception of the fact that man is, in each of his acts, more than the single act itself, grew the transcendental method. We shall have to make use of it if we wish to get beyond the merely superficial interrelations of our conscious activities and discover, at their roots, the fact of our dedication to death, which is their condition and reason. Discovering this dedication to death we shall also grasp the essential nature of man's death.

5. *Starting-Point for the Philosophical Analysis of Death*

Death is present in the whole structure of existence; therefore, any spontaneous activity of existence we may like to choose can be taken as the start of a philosophical analysis of death. There is, however, one act of existence which would seem to be peculiarly suited to this purpose, and that is the experience which philosophers since Plato have pointed out as the basic act of the philosopher, namely "wonder". This is an experience it is difficult to define. In it our existence is transplanted from its everyday experience and snatched away to the exalted realm of being. It can assume different forms. Buddha felt deeply the suffering of the world, and this set him off on a train of wondering reflexion. We are told of this young prince that he got up one day and "went forth into homelessness". His action is a symbol of the initial philosophical shock.

Augustine learnt of the death of a friend in a way which placed him with shattering suddenness before the ultimate questions of existence. "In the years when I first began teaching in my native town, I found, thanks to our common interest in learning, a true friend of the same age as myself and, like me, in the full vigour of youth. He had grown up with me from childhood; we had both gone to the same school, and played the same games. This friendship was very close indeed, ripened in the warmth of a like mutual affection." One day, however, death carried off this friend, and the emptiness left by his loss, opened up for Augustine the road to philosophy. "My heart grew dark for grief and pain, and everything I saw turned into an image of death. Even my native town became a torment, my parents' house an unbearable agony. Everywhere my eyes sought him out, nowhere did they find him, and all things seemed hateful to me, for they were not my friend. I became for myself a great riddle."[13]

It was by a mystical experience of which he informs us in his *Mémorial* that Pascal was summoned to the ultimate loneliness of wonderment, a solitary struggle, the violence of which is attested by those fragments of thought we call the *Pensées*. The ways and possibilities of making the ascent to philosophical wonderment are varied in the extreme. Once in a lifetime each of us reaches a point where solitude begins to grow and the daily world of experience vanishes into an uncanny remoteness. This is when the process leading to philosophical maturity begins, and it requires a good measure of mental courage if one is going to shoulder this transformation of the hitherto familiar world into one that is remote and uncanny, and to see precisely in this transformation the invitation made us by being.

What is the structure of this basic act of philosophy? Socrates' dialectic gives us a first indication. It shows us that there is, in philosophical wonderment, a twofold form of experience: Socrates evokes "wonder" in his partner by continually revealing that the apparently known is, in fact, unknown, only to go on from there and demonstrate that the unknown is, in reality, something long since known. This twofold element in the initial philosophical experience remains as a constant in all subsequent reflexion. Accordingly, philosophizing appears to be the mere re-enactment in all its dimensions of the basic act of philosophy. In every philosophical act of knowing the mind is catapulted out of its familiar world to the "unfamiliar" horizon of being. In the same moment, however, the knowing subject is directed back to the things of sense, but these meanwhile have become "unfamiliar", precisely because of the return of thought from its adventure with being. The tension between the being drawn away (i.e. the *ecstasis* of thought towards the infinite—which is what wisdom really is) and the being thrown back (i.e. the conversion to the contingent, which is the essence of foolishness) lies at the root of all philosophical experience. Accordingly, Plato is right when he says that, as a philosopher, one stands "midway between the sage and the fool".[14] Moreover, the famous two-way movement of the mind in Thomist thought (the *abstractio* and the *conversio ad phantasma*) is nothing but the translation into a metaphysical terminology of the tension between being caught up out of oneself (*ecstasis*) and being thrown back upon oneself of which we are conscious in the experiencing of philosophical wonder. We shall now attempt to open up the basic philosophical reaction of wonder by turning the keys leading to four forms of experience. In this way, we shall be laying the foundations for our analysis of death.

The first point at which we make the experience of philosophical wonder is, no doubt, *the shock with which we realize the uncertainty and mysteriousness of existence.* At the beginning of thought we always find an experience of this subjective uncertainty, dubiousness and indecision. Suddenly we are struck by some occurrence, perhaps something quite ordinary; a strange feeling of uncertainty comes over us and we feel all at once that we have lost our bearings in a world of insecure objects. This brings upon us a feeling of distress that, at times, can be so excessive that we cannot bear to be alone for one single moment. We know ourselves to be lost, and feel our own personal existence to be a mere plaything of inscrutable events, a solitary, aimless and isolated thing. Perhaps we can go on living in society, but we take part in events as if they did not properly concern us. Things have lost their name, almost even their form; it is as though they had no permanent individuality. In this abstraction of ours we make the fundamental discovery of an inner quality which seems to envelop all the actions, deeds and experiences we have mentioned. We are incapable of overtaking, of coming alongside our own deeds, of fully entering into our own acts, of stamping upon them our personality; we are incapable of being fully persons. Our own self constantly eludes us, and, it would seem, without our contributing in any way to this strange effect. The initial stirrings of existence never proceed really from ourselves; we simply follow them, as if impelled by something alien to ourselves.

Furthermore, to take up the point of the mysteriousness of existence: it is precisely in this impossibility of our ever catching up, an impossibility that forms the basis of our powerlessness both with ourselves and with the world, that we discover that our situation is worth questioning from the point of view of philosophy. In us there lives an unknown, in face of which we feel powerless; it is, therefore, something superior to us and seems to make our actions *a priori* of no account. As such, then, this unknown appears to us to be what we have always been aiming at in all our questionings. When, in our philosophical wonder, the fundamental powerlessness of existence is all at once removed from the periphery of consciousness into the centre of reflexion, our own existence is seen to be both bound up with impermanence and yet for ever breaking out of its provisional limitations; that is, it is shown to be something very questionable indeed: a disconcerting vacuum empty of meaning, and challenging us to a search for meaning. This is the beginning of philosophical reflexion.

There is a second point in our experience of philosophical wonder—*a feeling of uncertainty in the realm of the familiar*. The moment we feel insecure in our habitual system of relations with the world, we lose our grip on our mastery of the world as we had hitherto practised it. In the framework of the basic philosophical experience, there occurs the specific one Kierkegaard so impressively describes in his *Stages on Life's Way*—one's existence, on the level on which it has hitherto moved, comes up against a limit and perceives that on this level of existence life can progress no further. Courage must be found for a leap to a higher level, and this means that the whole system of relations with the world is involved in a crisis affecting all bed-rock principles. A new world is opened up to our existence, a world whose ways are untrodden, its promises untried and its hopes still uncertain. The leap itself, however, can no longer be put off, for the call of this new life becomes ever more pressing; so a man goes out from his old habitat and tries to find a footing in the unknown. The uncertainty experienced in philosophical wonder lies at a deeper level than the ordinary, everyday threats made to our existence, deeper than our ordinary experiences of failure. This need to make a leap into the dark reveals to us that there has been some obscure kind of loss, of existential loss. It is precisely in the urgency of this inescapable surrender of ourselves that we realize that the uncertainty of which we have now become aware has always been, without our knowing it, a component in all our actions, in the general tone of our existence, in our attitudes and our premonitions of the future. It (this uncertainty) has always been rising up from within us in varying emotional forms, assuming shapes, putting on masks or playing parts in our waking experiences, and still more, in our dreams. Whatever the different manifestations, one thing they all had in common—a feeling that we do not belong "here", that "somewhere" we have lost something, something very significant. What, we do not know and never have known. That is why we feel so much uncertainty about making the new leap in our existence, because we have always been so uncertain in our world, uncertain despite our superficial air of security in a self-made and forcibly maintained world-structure of practical utility. But, precisely in this uncertainty, we gain anew the knowledge that there is a sure guarantee. Even as we tried, amid the temporary expedients of our daily life, to build up for ourselves a safe situation out of small assurances, and palpable certainties, we were longing, all unconsciously, for a guarantee that would dominate them all. This quest for certainty is an unconscious return, a groping after something that lies far beyond the concrete forms of our search. We constantly strive to push our way across the mysterious boundary which runs through things, persons and events. We live in a constant expectation of infinite encounter and ineffable security.

The third point in the experience of philosophical wonder may be described as *the realization of the fact that our existence has no real home*. Our shock when we discover that our existence is such a questionable thing, our sudden insecurity in the world to which we are so accustomed, awaken in us secret anxieties, fears that take hold of us often without any apparent reason. We now discover that these anxieties conceal a mysterious feeling of not belonging. We remember how we had always lived with the consciousness that things are too remote, that the heart of man is too weak and that neither, therefore, could offer us a real, final home. All of which went to show our existential homelessness, to lay bare a fundamental vulnerability of our spirit. Again, it constantly happens that we throw ourselves into our activities with such enthusiasm that we find we have outrun them before they have really been completed.

We live in a state of perpetual overtaking, and that is why all we know, desire and feel, seems as if we had always known, desired and felt it: it strikes us as something we have already got beyond. Our existential urge is always thrusting forward past everything; it never wants to do more than just touch on things and then vanish into the unknown. An unceasing restlessness runs through all we do. It wants not only "more" knowledge, more fulfilment of desires, more satisfaction of feelings; it wants something "different". This restlessness marks the fundamental direction of the heart towards something transcendent, and in so pronounced a way that the presence of this transcendent something constitutes the essence of all we do. But since the transcendent is also the far-away, the unknown, always escaping our grasp, we find that we seem to be for ever on our way to meet an absentee. We can never possess it except as that which keeps its distance from us. The presence in and absence from our actions of this transcendent is what creates our subjective impression of being strangers, causing us to feel homeless always and everywhere. Our spirit is a foreigner: its nature is to be a reaching-out-further, an *en-route*-for, an expedition to find what is ever withheld.

It may be said that the fourth point where we experience philosophical wonder is *our consciousness of our own powerlessness*. We begin by making immense demands on existence and, then, do not feel strong enough to turn them into reality. The typically excessive demands of the weakling. This would seem to be the innermost feature of philosophical wonderment: a thoroughgoing sense of wonder at the significance of being and the insignificance of existence. This is precisely what makes it clear that the excessive pretensions and accompanying powerlessness of our existence jointly experienced in this philosophical wonder do not merely affect this or that particular in human life, but rather determine our whole attitude towards being. Excessively demanding and withal powerless—such is man. Excessive pretensions born for ever-renewed disappointments—this would seem to be the essence of our human estate as we experience it in philosophical wonder. It was said above that man in everything he does continually lies out ahead of himself, that he can never keep pace with his innermost longings, because these always thrust forward into the unattainable. This is another way of saying that man, of himself, has not the strength to be what, fundamentally, he already is. At the heart of this experience is a longing for one to protect him, care for him, console him and guide him. Man in his philosophical wonder finds that ever drinking he never ceases to thirst. He also finds that his thirst witnesses to the fact that there really does exist a never-failing spring of water.

This breakdown of wonder into the four points at which we experience it, merely develops what Augustine said about the basic act of philosophizing: "And I became for myself a great riddle", a strange being that feels itself essentially alien in all the situations into which life brings it; it is never able to enter completely into its own actions, and, therefore, lives in a constant state of frustration. It is homeless, because it is always carried away beyond what is at hand, beyond what it is accustomed to. It is a being that in its very powerlessness finds its hope a promise.

This experience is still obscure and the way in which we usually give an account of it is uncertain and non-technical in the highest degree. If we wish to bring out the essential pattern of all these presentiments, feelings, shocks and moods, we can say that the being we grasp in our philosophical wonder is divided in two; his figure is made up of contradictory elements. The two poles we find in him maintain a reciprocal and opposed tension and yet are inseparable. His inner fate is to be Something, and yet, at the same time Another in a state of opposed tension to this Something. This dualism appears first of all as frustration, discouragement, wretchedness, pusillanimity, thus showing that our existence is a subject, imprisoned thing. At the same time, however, it is a sign of transcendence, for the man who has realized the provisional character of his nature has, in so doing, risen superior to every merely temporary thing. Our insatisfaction is an indication of our mind's limitless aspirations. The man who recognizes that what he has accomplished is unsatisfactory, who so thoroughly tracks down his own helplessness; the man who has made the frightening experience of seeing his existence as a foreign body in a hostile environment, shows by all this that he is making higher demands. For a man can only become conscious of all this, if he has already in some fashion progressed beyond it. So then, in the basic philosophical experience of wonder our existence appears, at one and the same time, as hemmed in by the provisional and temporary, and as rising into the free realms of the final and definitive.

We shall attempt to apply the transcendental method to the examination of this dualism of our existence which we have grasped in our philosophical wonderment. In doing this we hope to discover that "dedication to death" which is a constitutive element in living, concrete existence.

6. *Summary of our Methodological Considerations*

In order to be in a position to undertake our analysis of death, we had to clarify various questions of method.

Firstly: *Is it possible for a temporal decision to be made in the very instant of a non-temporal transition?* This question is perfectly legitimate; for we have explained that the final decision which we have assumed as an hypothesis occurs neither before nor after death, but in death. On the other hand, however, this moment of death appears to be something non-temporal, a dividing line with no temporal extension of its own between a before and an after. Our reply to this first question was that the moment of death is a non-temporal transition whose very non-temporality, nevertheless, procures a passage in time from one state to another. The transition must be non-temporal, otherwise it would be impossible for the two moments—the before and the after—to interpenetrate one another and so form a compound and, therefore, temporal reality. Thus the soul has at its disposal a real "moment of time"—real, though altogether *sui generis*—for making in death its completely personal decision. This one moment is sufficient for the posing of a whole series of acts, for, in the moment of death, the soul attains to a new intensification of its temporal quality, and this enables it to realize in one flash its whole continuity of being.

Secondly: *How can we make any sort of philosophical pronouncement about death, when we never meet it as a direct experience?* Martin Heidegger gives us the answer to this question: death is essentially present in the structure of every living existence, and can, therefore, be grasped in the existent being itself at the point of intersection of the various pointers to death.

Thirdly: *Is there any way by which our thought can reveal the various pointers to death?* We can find such a way in the transcendental method which, setting out from concrete experiences, traces these back to the *a priori* realities on which they repose as on a foundation. We chose as our concrete starting-point the basic act of philosophic thought—wonder. From a thorough survey of the structure of existence disclosed in this fundamental act, we concluded that human beings live in a state of radical dualism. Our task now is to trace this dualism back to its transcendental causes, for, in this way, we hope to discover the figure of death in the structure of each living existence as it is.

II

THE PHILOSOPHICAL BASIS FOR THE HYPOTHESIS OF A FINAL DECISION

II

THE PHILOSOPHICAL BASIS FOR THE HYPOTHESIS OF A FINAL DECISION

From our methodological considerations two facts emerge. Firstly: Following Martin Heidegger's lead, we must seek the picture of death in the inner structure of living human existence. Secondly: We can discern this structure at the point where the dualism of our existence shows up, that is, in the basic philosophical experience of wonder. Since no one can stand alone with his thought, since the only thing capable of setting off a train of thought is a confrontation with truth as it works itself out in history, we propose to start off with four sections on the reflexions of philosophers who have probably had more intimate personal experience of our divided state than most. We shall not, however, limit ourselves to a merely descriptive account of their thought. We too shall endeavour to be creative and to progress further along the lines they indicate, taking their basic insights to their final consequences.

1. *The Presence of Death in the Will*

Maurice Blondel's suggestions in *Action* will be of assistance to us, enabling us to fill out Heidegger's conception of death by means of an analysis of the existential conflict in the will.[15] Blondel established that human volition always aims at infinitely more than a man in reality wills in any concrete act of the will. His philosophical activity was concerned with elucidating the transcendental causes of this conflict. In all his actions man seems to aim beyond and to will more than what he actually wants to attain. There is a radical absence of restraint in human volition, not only because in the concrete circumstances of life the possibility of realization is never secured except at the price of compromise with the absoluteness of the demand, but *fundamentally*, because right at the heart of volition there is this "More, more" of the driving urge. In every single act a man performs there seems to be at work a superabundance of power and light. The never-reduced inadequation between the urge and the end actually willed is an essential distinguishing mark of our existence.

Blondel has the great merit of having shown both the fact and the cause of man's inability to escape from this "ever wanting more". He investigated the question whether man can shut himself up in his actions, and whether the whole of existence is comprised in an identification and limitation of this sort, or whether the deeper volition, the elemental drive of human existence as such (*la volonté voulante*) did not compel man independently of any superficial conscious desire (*la volonté voulue*)—or even in opposition to it—to venture forth into more spacious realms. Man, after all, can only find rest when the will for the determinate object is capable of absorbing completely the full intensity of the will's elemental drive. In his search for the root of this elemental will and its insatiable appetite for more Blondel identified a drive which rises up in us even against our conscious will, imposed on us as pure necessity. In this way he discovered at the source of our activity a mysterious unknown that ever eludes our grasp and makes it impossible for us to stop and find contentment.

Blondel's real achievement, however, was the method which enabled him to perceive, on the basis of this contradiction, what is, in anticipation, asserted, pursued and—in some sort—attained in every stirring of volition. To do this he confronted conscious volition with the unconscious, unordered drive of the will. By a method of thesis and antithesis of the utmost scientific rigour—that is to say, following the direction of the drive only where no conscious volition could obstruct it—he was able to single out each of the elements aimed at by the drive from the very beginning. Blondel's dialectic, therefore, maps out one by one the different levels on which the person evolves, the regions in each of which it would like to settle down. Every time a man wishes to establish his lasting home in one spot, the thrust of his own being bears him on to fresh spaces. This experience of insufficiency does not come from any personal inadequacy. On the contrary, the more a man knows, the more he has, the more he is, the more conscious he becomes of the fact that he neither has nor is what he wants to have and to be. The pit seems to yawn ever deeper the more one attempts to fill it by satisfying the senses, the mind and the heart. Joy and sorrow, success and failure, possessions and their renunciation bring one to the same inescapable conclusion—however much the will may have attained by its own power, the actual achievement never corresponds to the desire from which it issued, the will has never willed itself completely and to the full. Whatever profit volition can show, in comparison with what it really willed the result is complete bankruptcy. At the end of the dialectical survey of the regions of consciousness, it is evident that man in every act of volition is really pressing on in an unordered manner towards a decision in which, when he has at last become one with his whole volition, he may be able to take his stand face to face with God.

God is, whether one feels able to call him God or not, the inescapable factor in every human action. He stands at the end of every road a man may set out to travel by. Flight from him is merely another form of running towards him and falling into his hands. Since the beginning he has always borne the weight of all human activity, and, as a consequence, he is inevitably brought into our field of consciousness. In one form or other he is always present to our mind's eye. In every volitional activity a secret bond of marriage is made between the human will and God. He is the transcendent being whom, through our fragmentary realizations, we constantly wish to overtake and confine within the prison of our deeds. Only at the point where we "catch up" with God, the constant aim, never attained, in all we do, can we actually be what we already are fundamentally and yet never succeed in being. Until that point is reached, Ernst Bloch's formulation of his "principle of hope" applies: "The decision has not yet been taken; even the question to be discussed has not yet been put."[16] Only in the act of our meeting with God can we catch up with ourselves and really become human beings.

If we examine the implications contained in these suggestions Blondel makes, it immediately becomes apparent that this total "catching up with God", our all-embracing *prise de position*, can be realized only in death. Until the moment of death our volition remains in its divided condition. Its individual acts are, until death comes, constantly being overtaken by the elemental drive of the will. God constantly evades anything we may do. He never becomes anything more than a distant goal for our actions as they constantly stretch out further and further towards him. If ever we come to a stop, he is not there; when we set out again, there he appears again. There can be no respite in our task of always going beyond the point we have reached, because God always stands further on. Any notion one may have—or may think one has—of him is merely provisional, a means of going further.

If, however, God can never be overtaken in this life, then it is equally true that our deepest self can never be overtaken by us. In our own activity there is something hidden which we are constantly pursuing as we try to overtake God. The two movements of existence, the unconscious drive towards God and the conscious realization, urge each other on. They attempt to reach each other, but never actually succeed in completely penetrating each other. But it is important to observe that they do pursue each other and are, therefore, constantly coming into contact in their dynamic thrust forward. In this mutual pursuit of the two movements of existence is contained an ontological exigency: sometime, somewhere, they must meet and coincide.

The entire movement of our being appears thus to sweep towards a single point of identity. Only at this point where all the threads spun by the strivings of our existence are joined in one tight knot of being, only at this point that we are never allowed to reach except in death —never in life—, only here can our existence attain a total identity of its original volition with the successive partial realizations of this volition.

This identity is, however, anticipated in every single act of existence. More than that, it is presupposed precisely in the mutual approach movements arising from the dynamism of existence. The whole movement, the constant overtaking of realization by an original existential plan of action, could not occur, if the reciprocal involvement of both was not present in us as the basis in reality for the movement of existence. Man is thus quite incapable of positing *the* act of his life in his lifetime, although he always bears this act within himself. Existence, drawn as if by a great magnet, is determined throughout its course by the field of this magnetic attraction. Everything in it strives towards a climax of free decision, or, to express the same thing in more precise terms: everything in it is constantly attracted by an ontologically pre-planned indication of the direction along which the decision to be taken must move.

One thing should here be emphasized: the final interpenetration of two elements—a primitive, irreductible impulse, on the one hand, and a realization by means of isolated acts, on the other—can only be accomplished as a decision, for the full positing of volition comprises also the total positing of freedom. The concentration of the person to a climax can never occur without the simultaneous concentration of freedom to a climax. Only in death can volition achieve full union in act with itself, by freely accepting (or rejecting) everything for which it had been striving already, right from the beginning. This makes it clear that human volition before death is never more than embryonic. Death is its birth. In its "prenatal" mode of existence the will learns the movements which will be indispensable to it on the day of its birth. In the course of its earthly development it is in training for the decisive and final act of the will. Death is thus the act of the will *simpliciter*.

That is the kind of way in which a Blondelism carried

further along the lines it had itself already indicated could give concrete form to the results obtained by Heidegger. Heidegger made it plain that death belongs of necessity to the actual living out of existence and that the origin of existence itself is to be found in a transcendental tension reaching out towards death. Blondel showed us how this projection into death takes shape in human volition. In every act of the will is contained a drive towards an all-embracing confrontation with itself and with everything that it had at all times, unconsciously and casually, posited in itself. But only in death can a total confrontation take place.

We have thus examined in one of its aspects the dualism of existence as we have grasped it in the basic philosophical experience, and' we have found the transcendental reason for this dualism to lie in the projection of existence into death as the achievement of full personality.

2. *Death as the Fulfilment of Knowing*

In the domain of the intellect our search for the figure of death can find an important indication as to the road to follow in certain suggestions of Joseph Maréchal's.[17] He confronted Thomist epistemology with the insights of German Idealism, particularly with those of Kant's transcendental philosophy, and discovered a fundamental dualism in human knowledge. Man's knowledge is, indeed, directed towards the world, but, at the same time, beyond it. In it there is always present an unbounded curiosity, an appetite for being in any shape or form. Even the most insignificant act of knowledge is stimulated by this appetite. That is why the entry of the mind into the world of sense can only be understood as a *fieri* of the spirit striving towards the absolute.

In this way, our reason knows more than it actually perceives. It lives in a constant *excessus*, in an *ecstasis* of thought towards God, and can perceive finite, sensory and earthly things only in the momentum of this infinite thrust forward.

This constant drive of knowledge towards God is, however, blind, so to speak. God is indeed "given" in every act of knowing, but he is never imagined, never represented. He is not seen, never appears in the line of vision of an *intuitio intellectualis*, but is implicitly affirmed in a vague, unconsidered way as the condition for the possibility of an objective knowledge of what is. This can even reach the point where a man denies God in a conscious act of reason, and yet, at the same time, affirms him implicitly, indeed cannot but affirm him, for a complete act is only possible on the basis of a real *ecstasis* towards God. It is by no means necessary that the implicitly and unreflectively "given" transcendence of the human mind, which in every intellectual act of knowledge points inarticulately to God, should be able to attach to its goal the name of "God".

Maréchal obtained these results by an exact analysis of the concrete act of knowing, an analysis which the limited scope of our present study makes it impossible for us to reproduce here. We shall attempt, however, to outline at least its essential structure.

To know means "to obtain possession of", "to assimilate". We take into the inner world of our existence something that is not ourself and give it a new being, the being known and illumined. The new being is, of course, essentially determined by this foreign, outside thing, but it is also entirely our creation. It is thanks to the mind that the light of being goes on in the object apprehended. Through the creative activity of our knowledge the foreign object receives a "light", that is, an extension of being. It attains an *ecstasis* into us. Its reality is elevated into our existence; it takes a place in our consciousness, and so attains the truest form of being: in it being and knowing coincide. In it being is "knownness", and as "knownness" it is being. This illumination, this lucidity has been created by us. But whence do we get this "light"?

When we try to grasp the nature of intellectual illumination, we observe a remarkable fact: illumination posits an affinity between the individual nature apprehended and the universe, and further than that, between the universe and God. We may express this more precisely as follows: there is present in our power of knowledge a light which is not limited to this or that, but is preordained to being as a whole. This structure finds its principal expression where the mind gives immanent expression to its knowledge, i.e. in its judgements. In each judgement we make we relate the whole of being to the individual object of our apprehension by the simple fact of saying that it "is". When it thus states that a thing "is", our thought stakes out a claim to the absolute expanse of being, to being in the undiminished totality of its significance; that means, to the world's being as a whole, and to that on which the world's being itself is founded—the infinite being of God. We pursue being through some small, individual part of the universe; we concentrate the universe in our one object and illumine the concentrated whole with the light of the Godhead. In other words, we strive after being in its whole extent, embrace the entire universe, and present God to everything we encounter by way of intellectual apprehension. Our intellectual apprehension is, therefore, and acts as an unlimited opening out on to the cosmos—and that implies an opening out to God; and all this in the embracing of some inconsidered part of reality.

There is a corollary to this: mind is a drive towards a return into oneself. Only if one condition were satisfied could our mind be completely in and with itself, viz. if it could represent to itself reflexively its own dynamism that carries it out towards God. Unfortunately, the way of complete self-reflexion is obstructed by our material state. Knowledge which is essentially dependent on the senses is the necessary condition of the embodied soul's self-presence (*Beisichsein*). From this arises the contradictory situation that human knowledge is, in the first place, a presence to another (*Bei-einem-andern-sein*), an immersion in the world (*Eingetaucht-sein-in-die-Welt*), and it is only this being torn away from oneself that provides a basis for the return into oneself, one's self-presence.

Our self-knowledge is essentially a return from the world of sense; self-presence for the human mind can be defined as "coming away from another" (*Von-einem-andern-herkommen*). Therefore, it is only in so far as knowing is directed towards representational, sensory objects, that the mind is conscious of itself and of that essential element implanted in its nature from the beginning—its appetite for the infinite. Only by moving into the world does man accomplish an act of knowing about God and his own reality.

Accordingly man is always a stranger to himself and never achieves that complete self-presence which should, nevertheless, constitute the very nature of the mind's knowing. However, in his entering into the world of sense, in this unremitting attempt to reach himself by hook or by crook, even at the cost of surrendering his self-presence itself, is contained a longing for an integral return to himself. In every act of knowing, the mind makes a desperate attempt to return to itself. It cannot relax its effort to move in the direction of its self.

If we follow through these suggestions of one of the most important thinkers in modern Scholasticism, we come to the conclusion that the first integral act of knowing will be possible for us only at the moment of death, when the mind is freed from the material principle. Only then can the mind come to itself immediately, without making a detour through the world of sense, without abandoning itself; only then can it come to itself and so posit in content and composition both its own nature and the infinite capacity that is an essential element in this nature. And since freedom also derives from the actual, fully realized expanse of the mind, this latter becomes completely free only when it grasps its infinite expanse—a reality always there as given—that is to say, in death. In reality, therefore, the case is the opposite of what Plato declared in his *anamnesis* theory: knowledge is in no sense a remembering of the timeless contemplation exercised in a pre-existent state; it is an anticipatory clutching at a possession—a holding—whose light can shine forth only in death. In this way, knowledge and freedom are ours only in the form of a preparatory exercise. Death is really a *dies natalis*, a day of birth for our mind, our first fully personal act.

This demonstration has enriched Heidegger's assumption of a projection of our existence into death by adding the precision of a second line of approach. In the light of Maréchal's reflexion we have examined the dualism of existence, as it is now revealed in our human knowledge, for its transcendental causes and lighted once more on an integral presence of death in concrete, living existence. In every individual act of knowing the human mind prepares for a perfect act of knowledge in which the integral self-presence of the mind—and therefore also its immersion in the absolute—becomes a state of being: the act of death.

3. *Integral Perception and Remembrance in Death*

The transcendental links we have been demonstrating are supplemented in an important way by Henri Bergson's reflexions on *perception* and *remembrance*. In two lectures given before the University of Oxford he summed up in these two points the results of his work in philosophy. By doing so he gave important hints for the elaboration of a theory of death.[18] On the basis of these two lectures we can determine still more exactly the discovery made by Heidegger that death is a fundamental aspect of concrete, living existence.

One of the principal insights of Bergson's researches into the conscious was his discovery of an essential dualism in our perception. There is in us a basically unlimited faculty of perception which, however, can function only as a straitened, constricted perception. The sharply circumscribed perception that is all we know in our daily life, arises from the fact that the requirements of ordinary action, our need to master our environment, reduce the field of our perceptive activity, presenting us with small pieces of the whole. Our ordinary perception objectifies from the world about us only such things as demand a vital answer, that is, the things about which we can or must do something. Our existence is constantly submerged under a flood of stimuli. The greater part of these simply flow through us without being arrested or noticed, while any stimuli of vital interest collide with the structures of our existence and are taken hold of. By an effort of the mind we succeed in narrowing down our conquest of the world, which, of itself, is absolutely unlimited. This is the only way we can lead a "practical" life.

This functional analysis reveals an inhibition on the part of the mind, which strives to limit its own horizon and turn away from anything that has no bearing on its day-to-day interests. From a ceaselessly inpouring stream of the most multifarious stimuli the sense-organs and above all the brain choose anything that is absolutely necessary for a profitable and vital orientation of life and, in this manner, carry out the selective activity of the mind. Otherwise our existence would be so taken up with the abundance of its perceptions that it would no longer be able to pursue its everyday course in the world. Thus we create for ourselves our small world of daily action by a metaphysical effort of the mind. Occasionally, however, the tension is relaxed, and we then begin to be dimly aware of deeper things.

Artists, we find, have an astonishing range of perception. They are relaxed people; they are less taken up than we are by the concrete side of life; they go about free as air and are, judged by our customary standards, absent-minded. It is precisely because the artist thinks less of turning his perceptions to useful account that he perceives a greater number of things. Obviously the world reveals itself to man only when he turns his attention from the practical, profit-seeking side of things and concentrates on what is of no "use" at all. This is the way in which is achieved a wholehearted conversion to reality. There is no other way to attain to the depths of intellectual knowledge: the mind must relax and abandon activity; it must even turn away from life, or, at least, give up that "attention to life" which is built into the structure of our existence. Calm and withdrawal from the world are, therefore, means to an integral possession of the world, switchpoints in the movement of our whole being, spaces for relaxation, and—as such—regions of unclouded perception of a world revealing itself in all its fullness.

A similar dualism was discovered by Bergson in our remembrance. On the one hand, our existence is completely open to its own past. Our life consists of an uninterrupted duration. It is a single sentence, begun on the first day of our consciousness, and nowhere divided up by full stops. Everything we have felt, thought and willed from our earliest childhood onwards, carries on into the present, pushing against the gate of consciousness. Our past lives on without any co-operation on our part, and survives in its integrity. Personal duration is a sustained melody which, from beginning to end, unbroken, goes on and on in the one, enduring present. Reality for Bergson is change, and change itself is an indivisible. That is why, for him, the past with the present forms a single whole. That means that it would be possible—and in conformity with the nature of human existence—for man to enter into full possession of his whole life in a single moment, to embrace it all in a *durée vécue*.

On the other hand, however, we observe in our consciousness a constant warding off of the past: "*Animus meminisse horret.*" The practical man concentrates on the future. The only part of his past that he wants to grasp is what will be of use in throwing light on the future. His interest is to push the past into the background and to permit nothing to come forward unless it is capable of strengthening a situation of practical action directed to the future. We accept into our present existence the useful experiences of the past and reject those that are of no use. This is what gives us the impression that the past is no longer there, that, indeed, it is not real. According to Bergson, this function of "de-realizing" the past is performed by the mental faculty we call "memory". In Bergson's understanding of existence the task of the memory is not to preserve such and such portions of the past, to store up experiences, to cause them to arise afresh from their state of "now-vanished", but, on the contrary, to exclude from our consciousness whatever in the past cannot be of use to us. Memory is seen, not as a place for preserving the past, but as a place from which it is to be excluded. The fundamental dualism of remembrance accordingly is this: the past lives on in us and remains present to us without any co-operation on our part; nevertheless, we turn away from it and live in an expectation solely preoccupied with the future, thus effectively de-realizing our past. The philosophical problem, therefore, is not how to account for the preservation of the past—it is constantly in us, of itself—but how to account for our filtration of it, our forgetting it and in part no longer perceiving it.

Our memory serves a number of purposes: it elevates into our consciousness the experiences that are of vital importance to us, simplifies them, turns them to useful account, makes a selection from among their abundance, but does not preserve them. In the brain nature has created a mechanism that directs our attention to the future and turns it away from the past. The reason why we do not live our past is that by our entire psychophysiological structure we are turned towards action and our self-interest. The beam of our growth towards consciousness is directed forwards. The "now", the moment in which we are, turns round upon itself and often does not perceive itself. As an immediately existent reality it is, as far as it is itself concerned, shrouded in darkness. Only when a now is waited for, is it not only lived *through*, but also lived *in*. The need to break out of the emptiness of the moment is for ever displacing the whole centre of gravity of our being, pushing it out ahead. We feel as though life could only acquire content and meaning from our future. However, could a man be sufficiently liberated from this expectation, he would be able to embrace the whole history of his existence in one undivided present.

Once more it is the artists and poets, the great virtuosi of absent-mindedness, the dreamers, the hopelessly unpractical people whose attention abstracts from the future and is really identified with the present. Immediately, at the waving of a fairy wand, the past becomes present for them. Their existence does an about-turn, steers consciousness in another direction and becomes capable of seizing the whole of life in one undivided present.

These insights of Bergson's contain the germ of an important philosophy of death, namely, that until death comes, we are never the masters of the movements of our being. Even when, on the surface of existence, we try to turn our faces to the present, the streams in the depths of our existence flow on constantly towards the future. It is not in our power to live fully *in* the plenitude of the moment. Only in death does man attain his moment of relaxation, the point beyond which he can go no further in the same direction, and where his existential orientation towards the future, his drive towards a concrete mastery over life come to an end in complete repose, and that, not only on the surface, but right down to the innermost fibres of his being. Our complete liberation, our thoroughgoing abandonment of our orientation towards a day-to-day future to be conquered through action, our surrender to the present—all these can accordingly only be "events in death". So death is the place of the total present.

In the relaxation of tension in death, then, we find we have reached the totality of reality (death as the place of integral perception) and reached a state of indwelling in our own existence (death as the place of identification with the past). Death is the place of total intuition. In death there spreads out a mighty vision of reality. Things acquire ultimate depth, cohesion and consistency, a never-suspected interrelation, an essential reality now grasped in unimpaired contemplation.

As though bursting from an exploding shell there arises before man the universe he has never previously perceived in its fullness, because he had until then moved about in it only as a man of action, never as a pure contemplative. Everything comes to life about him, a great surge of life carries essences and things along with it and establishes them in their true relations. At the same time the dividing line between present and past, drawn by our concentration of attention on the future, is effaced, and there is man, pure duration, in the fullness of his whole life. The past, which had lain in him like a motionless block of ice, thaws out and comes to life. This is the birth of the mind to its full possession of the world and to its own totality. Thus, in the act of death, the universe rises up in its full stature, and man enters into possession of his own undivided life. Out of his essential nature, now posited in its integrality, he can, now and only now, make his integral decision.

4. *Love as a Projection of our Existence into Death*

On the basis of suggestions made by Blondel, Maréchal and Bergson as regards volition, knowing, perception and remembrance, Heidegger's conception of death has now been further developed. Gabriel Marcel's research will enable us to open up the essential involvement in death of human love.[19]

Love and Death. In modern philosophy, indeed in the literature of all ages,[20] these two realities are seen to be intimately related, or better still, to be partial aspects of one and the same reality. Gabriel Marcel's Christian Socratism constantly circles round these two facts of our existence. The motto of one of his works is: *Le mythe d'Orphée et d'Euridice est au cœur même de mon existence.*[21] Marcel's analysis of love cannot be adequately presented in a few words. It rests on a phenomenological sub-structure of vast dimensions, and this cannot—from the very nature of things—be summarized. That is why we can here do nothing more than single out the essential elements in the unfolding of his thought. For the rest we would ask the reader to verify these thoughts in the light of his own experience and so make up for the absence here of a phenomenology.

According to Marcel, it is only through love that the individual, leading a life of dissipation and triviality, attains to the composure which allows of his being truly an "I". The opening up of our existence to meet another person creates our being. According to Marcel being is always being-with, and, more than that, being-with in love. "Being is being-with." In this metaphysical principle the accent is on the "with": our being is relationship, and the realization of our being is directed towards its complete identification with this relationship. Being is identification with its relationship and no longer remains being, that is, remains being only in so far as it is this relationship. In order to attain the being-with in love, our own existence must, so to speak, be given up; it must give up making use of the other person and treating him as a possession. Quite simply, man is meant to come to a personal fulfilment. His existence has not yet really come "to be"; it has first to be created in a community of persons, in the last analysis that means—in love; but love means powerlessness.

To love means, of course, to renounce any exercise of power and desire to interfere with, to "manage", to gain for oneself or to "possess" any other person. Love leaves the other person free; indeed love creates freedom in the other person; and in this case, creating freedom means self-effacement and renunciation. Love is realized in a great movement of self-emptying and, when once realized, is no more "our own" love, but comes to us from the other person; it is pure gift. In this gift and as gift we become what we "are"; that is, it is as gift that we begin "to be". The soul's trusting readiness to surrender itself and be at another's disposal (this key-concept of Marcel's—*disponibilité*) creates the possibility of love and, therefore, of being. In order to be, one must surrender oneself. This is the first basic insight in Marcel's analysis of love.

If we go on to ask what must really be given up, we get the answer: Everything must be given up in so far as it is not directed to the other person. It is not a matter of isolated points on which existence must reform in order to attain to love—the whole of existence must be transformed.

Everything in our human existence is dominated by

an urge to possess. The whole of existence is wrapped up in itself; it lives in a single, sinister circle of self-seeking. It is absolutely shattering to see how self-seeking insinuates itself into even the highest and purest motives. A rigorous introspection discovers even in the most selfless actions the roots of a self-seeking from which nothing in those actions is free. The human heart is the scene of a tense drama: wherever good in its purest form arises from within, it is immediately forced down again. Even the saints have found that their love of their neighbour was constantly threatened with collapse, that it was not love that was given to them, but the obligation to love. Their constant lament is this: one begins to give oneself selflessly, tries to seek only the welfare of one's fellows, to help those who are in need, to comfort the weak and afflicted, to live for another in love, and all at once one discovers that in all this lay hidden a dreadful falsehood, a hollow self-deception. Perhaps, after all, one has only been seeking oneself—even though it were in a sublime fashion! One was selfless because it gave one uplift; one gave help in order to find one's own satisfaction in another's gratitude; one comforted the suffering because in so doing one forgot one's own sorrow, because for a few moments one experienced one's own kindness of heart! Yet they, the saints, daily overcoming their own hearts, daily struggling against their cowardice, violence and selfishness—this means, in other words, in the daily practice of loyalty and fidelity —do try to build up their love anew, even though they know that they will always be too small to match its demands. Human love seems to be a complete impasse. The frightening ambiguity, the dualism of love consists in our never reaching the good in itself, but only the good that stands in a concrete relation to ourselves, "the good that is good for me". Volition in its ontic reality is precisely directed to its enrichment in being. The good aimed at fills the will with its being and forces the effort back into the subjective realm. So volition and love, even in moments of true surmounting of self, are surrounded by a kind of wall of subjectivity.

What actually happens to a person in those very rare moments in which the force of his love goes out—even though it be but fleetingly—towards another human being in such a way that this other is affirmed by him, and affirmed with all the fullness of his life? A situation is then dimly perceived as existing, and it is even attained for just a moment in a flaring up of the spirit, that can be described as follows: in the ecstasy of love no self-enrichment is sought or indeed experienced, even in a secondary way. If it were necessary and possible, the lover could sacrifice all self-enrichment to his love. This can go so far that his own love is not experienced in any way as "his", but is received in a spirit of unutterable humility as pure gift. As the old French saying has it: *"C'est moi qui te dois tout, puisque c'est moi qui t'aime."*

In these moments—even though it is not a lasting emotion—there occurs a surrender that is complete. The person has given himself, and held himself back only in so far as this was necessary for the gift offered. Whatever such a man still hopes for in life, he expects to receive for the sake of the other person. He hopes for something for himself so that he can give it to the other: *"J'espère en toi pour nous."* By this attitude the terrible self-centredness of existence is resolved, and man stands free as pure gift. Of course, such moments are fleeting and unstable. Existence falls back at once into itself and begins to fail in its self-giving. The wall of self is once more built up and must in loyalty be broken through again and again. Man is capable of delivering himself up to another in this way only in the most sublime, most generous hours of his life, and of "being" in this act of self-surrender for only a fleeting moment.

What, then, hinders the unfolding, the blossoming and the lasting of this fleeting love? Why, when it is attained, can it not continue? Marcel looks to corporeity for the explanation of this low content in being. Existence is inseparable from its embodiment. Things exist for it only in so far as they serve the "extension" of its bodily form. The corporeal, my body, however, is not "I". I "have", I possess a body, but I cannot simply be said "to be" my body. The body is, so to speak, my absolute possession (*avoir absolu*), and all that serves to extend my body enters into and establishes with me a relation of possession. Therefore, each act of existence must climb a steep slope if it is to ascend from "having–possessing" to "surrender–being". The fact that this latter state cannot be lastingly achieved is to be attributed to the basically low content in being of our existence. Through his corporeity man is immersed in the spheres of having and does not possess the strength to reshape this situation by the power of the spirit.

If we attempt to develop these ideas further, we come to the conclusion that the first possibility for changing the condition of having into a condition of being is presented at the moment of death. We make the transition to being only when our absolute possession, our body, takes leave of us. It would, however, be unwise to see in our deliverance from corporeity the sole basis for the disappearance of the condition of having (possession). In this moment the soul itself is completely exposed. Without the body, the "protection" provided for the soul even to its innermost recesses, is likewise no more. For, of course, having (possession) surrounded the soul with a protective shield, with a sphere of superficial security and immediately available assurance. Now these roots of having perish in the soul together with all the rest, and the soul itself somehow dies in this exposure. Since the preliminary condition of a complete surrender is, precisely, this exposure of the soul, the withering away of all having and self-centredness, the soul is at last able to produce something definitive, something that is no longer menaced by the provisional nature of having.

Accordingly the soul, at the same time, awakens to new possibilities of being. If the soul now accepts and affirms and acts out existentially its condition of ontological exposure, it never returns to itself again, but, in its affirmation of death, posits what it had in the loftiest moments of love already practised more or less—complete forgetfulness and surrender of self. Love and death have, therefore, a common root. The best love-stories end in death, and this is no accident. Love is, of course, and remains the triumph over death, but that is not because it abolishes death, but because it is itself death. Only in death is the total surrender that is love's possible, for only in death can we be exposed completely and without reserve. This is why lovers go so simply and unconcernedly to their death, for they are not entering a strange country; they are going into the inner chamber of love.

Thus Gabriel Marcel's discovery of the conflict between having and being in human love enables us to understand better Heidegger's assumption of the projection of our existence into death.

5. *Meeting-Point of the Historical Dialectic of Existence*

Our next consideration is intended to throw light on the hypothesis of a final decision from the point of view of a dualism inherent in history. It is based on the contemplation of the *double curve* of our life's graph which runs through the whole of our individual development in time, right up to our death. Taking his cue from the well-known passage in the Second Epistle to the Corinthians: "Though the outward part of our nature is being worn down, our inner life is refreshed from day to day",[22] St Augustine had already, more than once, drawn attention to this thought. In Augustinian anthropology it would be a mistake to understand the antithesis "outer–inner" as being equated purely and simply with the other antithesis "body–spirit". These terms denote complete human realities which include and are firmly fixed in both spheres—the corporeal and the spiritual. On this point at least Augustine was further from Platonism than is generally assumed. If we try to investigate Augustine's indications for ourselves, we do, as a matter of fact, find, running through all the stages of a man's destiny, through all the apparent absurdities of life, two lines, two curves of existence which do not cut until death. If we follow out these two movements of our existence, we shall observe that death itself appears at the point where they meet and intersect.[23]

The first curve of existence reveals an *irreversible exhaustion* of our vital reserves. At the moment of fertilization existence begins, entering upon a phase which at first rises steeply; then it passes through the further stages of growth and consolidation. In this period existence undergoes a progressive differentiation and specialization of its inherent potentialities. Then come the phases of withering, of decline, and finally the fateful stage of decease. So then, man, as he evolves, presents a series of forms: he is an ovum, an embryo, a child, a youth, an adult, a middle-aged man and an old man.

At the beginning his organism is the scene of an explosive bursting forth of forces. These are set to work generously, recklessly squandered in fact. Physiologically man lives at the beginning in a sort of headlong rush. Various observations, for example, the experiments carried out by Alexis Carrel and Pierre Lecomte du Noüy to ascertain the rate of healing of a superficial wound, have given us a fairly exact insight into the immensely quick rhythm of physiological time at the beginning of life.[24] But this abounding vital energy slowly begins to decrease, and man starts nibbling at his reserves. The vigorous drive of youth begins to slacken, the vital forces flow ever more scantily. One becomes conscious of the limits of one's own strength; one feels weighed down by the burden of work. By a skilful use of his powers and by a rational co-ordination of his actions a man is able for a time to compensate his losses, but slowly his existence is overcome by exhaustion. The body-structure, so elastic at first, becomes brittle and rigid and loses its power of adaptation, till in the end it breaks like a stick of chalk. At the same time there also takes place a change to existential rigidity: the psychic structures also grow more and more inflexible. Such typical phenomena of old age as awkwardness, obstinacy and stubborn narrow-mindedness are more and more in evidence. An old man loses strength, freshness and elasticity, not only of body, but usually of mind too. The whole existence gives an impression of lifelessness, fossilization and rigidity. All that remains of the experienced reality of the mastery of life is a settled formula, a piece of flotsam which the waves of change have thrown up against the cliffs.

The ageing man is encompassed by a host of still-born potentialities—what his life might have been. At the end he sees with terrifying clarity that life, all along, had been facing him with a choice and that he, by the very fact of pursuing the course he did pursue in his lifetime, condemned his other potentialities to death. He robbed himself of the sight of those regions through which other ways of life might have led him. The feeling of a loss which can never be made good takes possession of his soul. Full of anxiety he becomes aware of the fact that the fullness of life has escaped him. From this again springs a longing to keep hold of such lasting things as he may have created. He feels himself to have been cheated of what is most personally his and, like a miser, holds fast what he can still call his possessions. It is, however, a fundamental principle of our sojourn in this world that we have existential possession of things only in one circumstance, namely, when we use them and dispose of them *with our mind*, when we transform them from within.

Possession is, in human life, an act of the mind. As soon as the inner power of conferring forms on things slows down, or indeed dies altogether, things return, as it were, to their essentially unresponsive, inanimate existence as things. In an existential sense property ceases to be possession when it can no longer be made our own by an act of the mind. The ageing man, therefore, perceives with horror that the world is slipping from his grasp, because he lacks the strength to hold on to it by a constantly renewed mental act of re-possession. Accordingly he begins to cling fast to whatever he can still clutch in his trembling hands, until at last death deprives him of anything he still had left.

So then, life's energies follow, in body and mind, a falling curve of increasing rigidity and diminishing efficiency. All that concerns the "outer man": achievement, success, self-assertion, the mastery over and disposal of things and men—all this follows this downward curve. Yet at the same time, there opens up the possibility of an inner ascent. The "inner man", that is, man as plenitude of significance, power of illumination, wisdom, genuineness, transcendent transparency, breadth of heart, purified, refined human understanding, and withal, as completely integrated experience—in a word, the man who can become the interpreter of spiritual meaning, gnaws away at the strength of the "outer man". The more the "outer man" disintegrates, the purer is seen to be the possibility of an ascent to interiority.

Therefore, the "outer man's" supply of energy need not necessarily disappear unused. It can be transformed into energy of another kind, capable of following its own *curve of existence opposed to the first.* The laws governing this second development are interior ones, a duty laid upon our liberty. They can be a total failure, or again, they can be realized to varying degrees of perfection. In any case, they bring the necessity of our being into touch with our freedom. When a man takes this direction determined from within, the energies of the "outer man" are transformed into a new state of being, turned into spirit. All through the different stages of life the possibility is opened up of becoming one's self, of widening one's sphere of existence, of positing one's freedom. We now propose to give a brief outline of these three possible determinations of the rising curve of existence.

Firstly: *Achievement of an independent centre of being.*

The curve of the "outer man" imposes on our being a definite rhythm. Through the different stages of life man meets increasingly with crises, with new trials. The minor difficulties of one stage, at first overcome with hardly any effort, gradually increase and from them there comes into being an existential emergency, which must be faced with spiritual forces. Romano Guardini distinguishes five such crises: birth, puberty, experience, climacteric and dissolution. These moments of heightened involvement are the product of the course of existence traced by the "outer man", and confront the "inner man" on each occasion as it arises with the necessity of making a decision. He has to revise the modes of his perception, insight and attitude to the world; he has to free himself from a superseded mode of existence, save what is of value in the old phase of life for use in the new phase, and by so doing give it an increased content of spirit.

Life does not stop to ask our opinion or our leave. We are driven out of our well-organized situation. Suddenly there comes a point beyond which we can go no further by adhering to the old rules. Plans for a new state of being must be made and life faced in a new condition of independence.

In each of these crises can be rediscovered to a certain degree the primitive image of all emergencies, namely birth. In that primitive experience the whole organism had to readapt itself completely to save itself from immediate death. The lungs opened with a cry of distress. The tiny being had to begin to assure all by itself the maintenance of an equable body temperature, to absorb nourishment directly, and so on. This means that for the first time it went through a whole series of experiences which would accompany it throughout its entire life—the wonder of tender caresses, the delightful feeling of satisfied hunger, the light and colour of the world. The same thing occurs as a spiritual experience in every crisis. On successfully surmounting the crisis of puberty a man awakes to the experience of the absolute, an experience that will enable him to make the venture of establishing human contacts. From this comes a whole constellation of values: honour, courage, responsibility, truthfulness, reliability, and so forth. Thus he grows slowly on towards a sense of responsibility, and gives expression to the absolute in his mental make-up by a show of youth's refusal of compromise and joyful acceptance of self-sacrifice.

It is precisely from these absolutist attitudes that later a new crisis arises: the crisis of experience. In this a man attains an inner maturity, a manner of existence which may perhaps be less interesting and revolutionary, but which is on the other hand solid and firmly rooted in earthly reality—he becomes a responsible citizen. Active thought, feeling and volition all come together in one spiritual nucleus. In this process the solid cohesion of the personality develops. Man becomes capable of establishing new and defending already established values, of exercising power justly and loyally, of creating a life-communicating tradition. In this period of creative achievement the responsible man takes more and more burdens on himself and, doing so, often does not notice how his vital forces are deserting him.

In the end, the falling of the "outer man's" curve of existence becomes plain to see. A new emergency arises: the crisis of the climacteric. Life loses its freshness, its novelty, its stimulus. The poverty of existence is revealed. If this deeply sobering realization is mastered from within, if life with its burdens, despite all its disillusionments, is affirmed from a fund of inner seriousness, a new manner of existence comes into being: the middle-aged man. His attitude is one of discipline and self-denial. He loses his illusions: he learns to face up to disorder, suffering and inevitable frustration, to accept them, to conform himself to them, and yet, to achieve something of lasting value.

Finally, the fact of decline makes itself felt with elemental violence and brings about the crisis of dissolution. The strength of the "outer man" begins to ebb away. This makes possible the most decisive renewal of the "inner man", the deepest spiritualization of life. Overcoming this final impoverishment there emerges the old man, the wise man, the elder, whose whole strength is spirit, deriving from a composure we can really call saintly. Perhaps such men say little, or at any rate little of importance, but by their simple presence they transform the complex of existence and make it transparent. Their "act" of essential being is the spiritual transparency of the realized meaning of existence. An aura of strength surrounds them, not a strength that has its origin in mere deeds, but one that breaks into their existence from another sphere without any collaboration on their part, as the strength of unsullied limpidity and unclouded understanding. Through the utter simplicity of their existence they become the interpreters of the spiritual meaning that lives in others. The hidden, near-divine shape of human existence emerges. They are men to whom the vast spaces of infinity lie open. In their eyes shine gentleness, tolerance, harmony and a tranquillity of infinite understanding—that look that Oskar Kokoschka was able to catch in his extraordinary portrait of Professor Forell. These men have transformed all the energy of life into person.

At the end comes yet another crisis which is not really

a crisis, but *the* crisis of life, a final emergency which, this time, one cannot observe oneself—death. We can, however, get some idea of it by pursuing still further the general trend of the dialectic of the "outer" and "inner" man, by observing the tendency towards coincidence of the two curves of existence. With every diminution of his vital forces, a man kept discovering in himself a new potentiality for being, more completely, a person; and, at the same time, in the wake of all the crises already overcome, an independent centre inside existence itself was slowly coming into being. If we prolong the two curves of existence as far as death, we observe the following result: the personal element in its fullness—in other words, the inner man—can only emerge in death, when the energies of the outer man disappear. The whole dynamic force of existence is then transformed into person and the man can arise in the completely untrammelled statement of himself as man.

Secondly: *Widening of the existential environment.* Since the person in its continuous development cannot be detached from its whole position in the world, our first investigation must be completed by a complementary consideration. As the person develops, a steady widening of the existential environment takes place, and accordingly a widening of the inner sphere in which we live. The first widening of our existential *milieu*—and one that burst its whole framework—occurred at birth, but how small this new world is! Its boundaries are set by the helplessly outstretched arms, the mother's lap, the edge of the cradle. After being weaned the child experiences the world of varying forms of nourishment. Reaching out ever further it discovers by slow degrees its own body, comes upon things of the world about it. Then it leaves the confined environment formed by the cradle and begins to crawl about in the nursery. It is already living as a member of a family, and beginning to understand a whole new world of meanings. Words, gestures, mimicry form round the tiny person an environment that already extends into the world of the mind and spirit.

Then follows the great voyage of discovery through the different rooms, up and down the stairs, into the garden and out into the streets. These experiences stock the imagination with a wealth of material. From the scraps of experience the child picks up, it then constructs a world for itself which is already governed by metaphysical laws—the associative logic of the fairy-story.[25] More and more the little human comes into contact with a larger world dominated, it may be, by unsympathetic and terrifying factors; it comes into touch with the sphere of relationships with other, but unknown, human beings. Meanwhile it has discovered that even in the surroundings of home and family there are certain spheres of intimacy among the grown-ups, from which it is excluded. Through experience the child gets to know the neighbourhood, then gradually the town, which is part of a whole, only vaguely guessed at, that is called "this country", which, in its turn, is included in a mysterious unknown, the entire world. Among its playfellows the child is, even in the most favourable instances, treated as no more than an equal. The privileges of being protected disappear. This stimulates the search for a new intimacy, and so the child opens up to the experience of friendship, which will later give access to the sphere of love.

So the young person slowly learns to recognize what a person is in its uniqueness. He perceives, at first indeed only vaguely, that he is, in a person, brought up against something sacred and mysterious. If he wants to make of his self-donation something entire, unconditional, irrevocable, he finds that the other person is quite incapable of receiving this donation in its entirety. A residue of love always remains, a longing not satisfied by the most intimate association; it pours forth more and more powerfully from the lover's heart and draws it towards something unknown. At first in love the search for personal happiness, for sensual enjoyment and an agreeable life is predominant. When this period of intoxication is past, the lovers face the task of overcoming their egoism and helping one another to attain to a complete humanity. In this context grows the perception of that absolute that arises from within a donation which is slowly being transfigured. The person perceives that his existence is a thing surrounded by the sacred, and this endows the world with a new dimension extending into the metaphysical depths of the world's being.

A similar extension of one's relationship with the world occurs in the sphere of professional work. At first a man is aware of his own power to transform things; he perceives the creativeness of his activity. He interferes with nature and, in his hands, world energy takes on new forms and a new countenance. Thus he comes to possess a down-to-earth, clear mind, an eye for essentials, a sense of reality he had not known before, a gift of going straight to the point, self-discipline, a sense for orderliness—qualities of the truly creative man. His own experiences and subjective values seem to him, in the light of this new perception, to be unimportant and uninteresting, compared with the great task to which he wants to devote himself. This is, then, an attitude of totally untheatrical courage in facing a world which has yet to be created.

Slowly, however, he notices—and the experience will play an ever more decisive part in his life—that inwardly he is not equal to his task, that his dream always exceeds his achievement, that he does not possess the power to perfect the world, rather, that the world in its essence is not perfectible by human means. Beyond this imperfectible world and beyond his own longing for creative perfection he experiences another world, which will come not from human hands alone but from God's grace. In a whole series of such experiences a man enlarges his existential horizon, at first only quantitatively, but later in a qualitative dimension also. It is precisely at the point where a man experiences existentially that he is not equal to the world and can no longer encompass it that it begins to grow into a metaphysical thing. At the end of his life a man's formative powers abandon him each day a little more surely. His existential environment shrinks: he can no longer make his way about the town, then the house and lastly his room. Nothing is left for him finally but the easy chair or the bed where he will before long breathe his last. But his experience of the depths contained in the world continues, indeed it grows as the available physical space shrinks. At the end the old man holds a world of the spirit in his trembling hands, though these are powerless to grasp the outward, physical cosmos.

If we attempt to project into death the dialectic between the shrinking of the physical cosmos and the enlargement of the spiritual world, and to carry them on to the point at which they intersect, then we get some idea of what really may happen in death. Existential space in the physical sense shrinks until nothing is left, but at the same time the spiritually perceived world grows into the infinite. The boundaries of the spiritual world are pushed back and man stands before a perfected universe, now seen in its real, essential depth. This universe now becomes his final path; along this he has to make his courageous way to God, daring all in one last, reckless step.

Thirdly: *Positing of freedom.* An infant is determined, even in its tiniest stirrings, by vital reflexes. By birth the human being enters a sphere of "being-with", of community, in which he tries out his first conscious movements as a preliminary exercise of his free, independent individuality. At the same time, new determinisms arise. To the physiological conditions of existence there are now added the psychological determinisms of education, and of family, social and cultural influences. In the first years of a child's education a mass of predeterminations arise which reach deep into the unconscious. Psychic complexes are formed which a man has to bear with him all through his life; prejudices, standards, modes of behaviour are adopted and stabilized as mechanisms for action. Thus the material accumulates from which one is to construct one's world.

As the personality, still bound up with the world nearest to it, begins to assert its independence, it discovers that all these predeterminisms require a constant putting in order and purifying of the person itself. In this way arises the task of building oneself up into an independent being from one's biological, family and social roots. Man begins to work on himself, to exert his capabilities in the service of a task, and measure his actions against an ideal. He becomes capable of taking an objective look at his body, his works, even his life. All this demands self-mastery, discipline, sacrifice; but through these there grows out of the stock of innate and acquired dispositions a pattern of existence. This is no longer a chance meeting of extra-personal influences, but a freely achieved individuality.

He begins to find his feet, to take responsibility for himself; in a word, to be free. He becomes "the child of his own works", he creates himself. In this way, his relations with the world about him are at once changed, as if chains had been struck from his limbs. The constraint is ended and the living person rises to a freedom which, till then, had been denied him, a triple freedom: to examine the world, to classify it, and to dispose of it at will. Man begins his creative activity in the universe. He discovers what an undreamt of part his own subjectivity plays in forming the world. He begins a creative activity in the technical field: he begins to carry through his own ideas in industrial and social contexts, to form scientific hypotheses, to give expression to his inner resources in the form of mature art, to determine freely his particular *milieu*, to formulate—perhaps not very consciously, but none the less effectively—his own interpretation of existence—in a word, to reshape the given elements of the world in his own original fashion.

Step by step he acquires greater freedom in relation to the world about him and to himself. His creative activity is also at work within his own person. Certain features of the personality he has become are accepted without question, others he develops consciously, others again he rejects, slowly excluding them from the pattern of his personality. In this process his freedom grows and he begins to be what he has made of himself. Thus, what is conserved no less than what is taken from elsewhere is interiorized, remodelled and reassembled on a new plan. From the facts of existence and the surrounding world an inner sphere of being a human being is built up. This inner man is brought about by a never-ending daily application, on the treadmill of duties, annoyances, joys and difficulties. From these insignificant actions freely performed, the great decisive freedom is built up—freedom from oneself, freedom to view one's own existence from outside. The external freedom of action diminishes as time passes, as the vital forces slowly but inexorably fail. At last man appears in the fullness of his days and works, and in the inestimable possession of a definitively achieved deliverance. From the crowded days and years of joy and sorrow something has crystallized out, the rudimentary forms of which were already present in all his experiences, his struggles, his creative work, his patience and love—namely, the inner self, the individual, supremely individual creation of a man. He has given his own shape to the determinisms of life by a daily conquest of them; he has become the master of the multiple relations that go to make him up, by accepting them as the raw material of his self. Now he begins to "be".

If we try to grasp the immanent dynamism of this process—by this we mean the efficacious draft outline of a condition which, though not yet realized, is already operative and significant—we observe a tendency: man experiences an urge to posit himself and, by this means, to become completely free. He cannot, however, attain this, for he never has anything but the "material" at hand to work on, that is to say, his own existence with the potentialities and limitations it offers, his character, his contingent situation in the surrounding world. Only then can he really posit himself fully when he can call into existence, out of the bases of his own being, a body (no less), and a relationship with his surroundings and his neighbours. To do this he must previously lay aside his old relationships, both with the body and with the world. This again means that the condition for complete freedom and complete positing of self—and that is, basically, the same thing—is a farewell to the "outer man", that is, death. Accordingly death would seem to be the place of total freedom and, therefore, the condition in which man can himself produce his outer aspect, his own corporeal state.

If we combine the insights we have gained in the course of these three considerations, we get from them a picture of death which coincides exactly with the picture we outlined in our hypothesis of a final decision. In death man becomes for the first time, and finally, a person, an independent and spiritualized centre of being. At the same time he enlarges his existential environment to the dimensions of the world seen in all its depth. Finally, in himself, in the possession of his complete personality, he can produce a corporeity of his own and so be free, i.e. "self-posited", right down to the most hidden fibres of his reality.

6. *The Previous Sampling of Death Found in Poetic Experience*

Poetic experience has a good claim to consideration as a further link in the chain of our proof by partial indications.[26] It seems clear that in the personal experience and act of "poetic creation" existence enters into the dimension of death. Accordingly, it seems probable that an exact analysis of Hölderlin's "dwelling as a poet" may cast some light on Heidegger's assumption that existence is projected into death.

Hölderlin saw that "man dwells on this earth as a poet", meaning that poetry is the basis of life, the mode according to which man is called to live in proximity to the nature of things, to "dwell" in the earth. It is only thanks to the values created by poetry that our world can ever become a dwelling-place for existence. But what is poetry? It is the creation of being by means of words, the salvaging of true reality from confusion, the establishing of existence on its real basis; in short, the experience of the presence in our existence (in its integral reality) of death, and a sampling of death as our fully personal, perfect accomplishment.

In order to prove this, let us examine the dualism inherent in poetry for its inner dynamism. On the one hand, of course, poetry is the creation of a new relationship to the world, defining as such a real proximity to the world. On the other hand, it thrives in existential isolation, supposing a withdrawal from the world as fundamental as it is unique, a separation nowhere else attained. To these two attributes of poetry must be added as an expression and basis of them both, a third: poetry is a crying out for a presence of God. In the dialectical confrontation of these attributes of poetry we hope that the shape of death will appear.

Poetry, then, is the creation of a new relationship to the world, establishing thus a real *proximity to the world,* unique in its kind and nowhere else attained. R. M. Rilke in his *Notebook of Malte Laurids Brigge* described poetic creation as the conservation and fitting together of a whole life's scattered experiences of meaning and lucidity.[27] To be a poet, therefore, means to separate from their context of day-to-day living the really important experiences one makes in the course of life, and thus to express in a tightly interwoven web the essential proximity of things, happenings and persons as we have grasped it in the most lucid moments of our being as men. By this means one salvages whatever is light, meaning, personal enrichment, openness, from the surrounding confusion and makes of it all new being.

In itself our existence is non-transparent. Human actions are never more than attempts to reach up to what far transcends the individual actions. Only rarely, in moments of great spiritual intensity, do we ever succeed in really encountering things and ourselves; and even these bright encounters in the real meaning of the word are fleeting and haphazard. They are already overtaken and lost before we have had time to savour them fully. Our experience of true reality is only a piecemeal thing, spread over very different and completely unrelated points in our whole movement of existence. In dark unknowing we grope forward along ways which are only seldom lit up by a lightning-flash of experienced significance, only to be plunged again immediately thereafter into the murky darkness that is the landscape of our existence. Out of this life of confusion poetry rescues the significant moments. It links up the scattered pieces and moments of true existential reality and out of them creates a new world relationship; this means a new cosmos. Out of the scattered pieces and broken sherds of our experience of significance poetry creates a warm centre of things, a home made of lucidity, openness and honest reality. This new world is not only fairer, deeper, more alive than the world of our day-to-day living; it is essentially "more"; it is what, in the confused dissipation of our existence, we can never experience for any length of time and never keep for ever.

So then, in poetic creation we can perceive at work a dynamism of existence. In an act of total positing of the self and of the world, its aim is to create out of the material of unreality something that will be definitive and truly real, something lasting, capable of gathering up into one the experiences of significance and lucidity; and this it does by enlarging them to the dimensions of the absolute. This is what our existence is attempting in the fact of "dwelling as a poet".

Secondly, however, poetry is our act of uncompromising isolation supposing a real *remoteness from the world*, unique in its kind and nowhere else attained. The storing process described above is carried out in the poet's isolation. An essential prerequisite for the salvaging of the truly real from among its surrounding confusion is that the individual existence should know about both the reality and the confusion. Accordingly poetic activity can only occur in a frontier position. Existence must have its taste of the transcendent and, at the same time, be flung back into the world here below. It is as a foreigner, waiting expectantly at the frontier, that the living existence produces poetry.

This frontier position, this disquiet occasioned by the allurement of two worlds, is the famous "poetic melancholy", but melancholy, after all, is merely the experience of the simultaneous proximity and remoteness of a transcendent reality. Basically it is the existential realization of an ontological difference: existence reaches into being and at the same time understands that it is something far removed from being. In melancholy man takes his place right in the midst of the difference. Accordingly anything at all that comes into contact with melancholy receives the light of fullness of significance and the light of intelligibility; but it is also simultaneously thrust back into its shrouding veils and lost in the night of absence of significance and the night of unintelligibility. This experience is a condition *sine qua non* of poetic creativity. In it there arises from the depths of the soul the presentiment of a fundamentally new element hidden in the bosom of the old. The substance of this "attitude of melancholy" is to be found in the poet's isolation. The spirit gathers itself as melancholy, as experienced difference, into a single gesture of farewell. It takes itself afar off in order to be nearer to the world. The nearness of things is made really near only through their remoteness. "Something kind must be near, close to me from afar," says Hölderlin in *Menon's Lament for Diotima.* All hiding is revealing, all dark is light, all concealment is beauty, all retirement is presence. In the poet's isolation the two *rapports* are mutually ordained the one to the other. Only in this dialectic of the proximity that is realized in remoteness can the phenomenon poetry occur. With a gesture of farewell poetry lets things go free. In this farewell, in this departure for the faraway, the world manifests its truest reality. We abandon things, we give up all idea of seizing and grasping. That liberates the world and makes it possible for mysterious and transcendent realities to rise up. The world can bestow its deepest content on us only when we step back in farewell, not if we endeavour to draw near and embrace it.[28] If, therefore, the endeavour of "dwelling as poet" is to enable the world to appear in all its plenitude, i.e. to experience all the world's nearness, then its endeavour is also to achieve a complete isolation from the world, a remoteness of self-restraint.

A third attribute of poetry must now be added to the preceding two: poetry is a *crying out for a presence of God.* The final fruit in words of poetic activity, the poem, expresses the new world discovered in the poet's isolation and lends it being through the poetic word. But what is the poetic word? It is "speech", effective speech. It has the power to cast a spell on things, to enlighten world relationships, to render the world translucent to an infinity, and to cause many sounds to blend together in one harmony. In a real poem only words like these have their place. The purer the use of these words, the more closely knit the poem. The closer these pure poetical words come together, the more simply they touch one another, the fuller the reality created by poetic speech.

Nevertheless, the poet's words, no matter how effective they may be, can only bestow on what is suggested in his poetical speech a content as "word", never a content as "being". Accordingly all they can do for us is to open up doors to the infinite. The poet's effective words, therefore, are words of longing. The poet's word is the unadorned calling after that which those who are ever surmising expect and long for, and in it the thing called for is already present. In the call poetry makes, what is called and summoned is the very thing that can make the call itself "effective", or in other words, "creative of being". But what is it, after all, that poetry is supposed to create? What is aimed at and projected in poetic creation is something that surpasses our existence of confusion. It is the Other, that something that in its being transcends him who makes the call. This means that what is called and summoned in our longing—what is, indeed, called to our help—is the transcendent, and this is, in the final analysis, the one and only effective word, the Word of God. In this way then, our existence moves dynamically, in poetical experience, into the presence of God and proclaims that it contains a sampling of the total, complete presence of God.

Let us now bring together the basic characteristics of poetry and we shall discover at the meeting-point of the inner dynamisms inspiring poetic creativity a statement on the subject of human death. In poetry a drive towards an integral proximity to the world is at work; but this proximity can only be attained through isolation. If the proximity is to be really complete, the isolation must also be complete; but the absolutely complete realization of isolation is death. Only in death do the little farewells of our existence coalesce into a departure that has the density of being and is, therefore, total. Furthermore, its isolation is at the same time that remoteness in which the total proximity of the world comes about, so that in death the unconditional proximity to the world is also given to us. This proximity consists in the establishing of a new relationship with the world, in a total trans- or re-formation of existence. This new positing, seeing it produces a transcendent, must be realized in a total presence of God. So that, in conclusion, our analysis of the inner dynamism of "dwelling as a poet" has produced for us a picture of human death: death is that process whereby the integral creation of the world is achieved starting from the presence of God.

7. *Accomplishment and Perfection of the Kenotic Actualization of Existence*

A final link in our chain of proof by partial indications is an attempt to obtain an even more exact idea of death from the most radical of all conflicts within existence. The basic functions of existence are comprised in *kenosis* (self-emptying),[29] *the dialectic of destruction*, the successive stages of which are being, non-being and then being again. From its initial content of being the living existence, with a gesture of self-surrender, moves over to a denial of that same content of being, reaching in this way a new plenitude of being. Only by surrendering ourselves, can we be filled. We distinguish four basic aspects of kenosis in our existence. This will enable us to understand the supreme kenosis of life—death.

The kenotic movement can be seen, to begin with, on the level of human consciousness. The closed circuit of increasing self-consciousness comes into being by the fact that a given existence abandons its "being-in-itself" and moves on into "extraneity". We are not essentially, by nature, at home in ourselves; we can attain ourselves only by our acts; our acts can be performed only in a state of tension set up between the knowing subject and the object confronting him. As a result, the consciousness reaches the "I" only by a detour through the "non-I". We know ourselves only when we leave ourselves behind. We have to burst out of the closed sphere of the subjective and expose ourselves and perceive ourselves in our content as "others", precisely in the process of identifying ourselves with, and losing ourselves in, what is objectively given. By the accepting into our interiority of what is exterior, we are enabled to experience our interiority. The consciousness, by interlarding itself with foreign matter, begins to be a consciousness.

The kenotic attitude is even clearer in the case of the urge to *love*. A good deal was already said on this aspect in our exposition of Marcel's analysis of love.[30] So now we can be brief. We cannot begin to be a person until we learn to give up clinging to our self, when we begin, for better or for worse, to hand ourselves over to another. The nature of love is to be a surrender even of one's very being, a removing of oneself out of the centre of one's affirmation of existence, a transferring into the other's being of the centre of gravity of one's existence. This surrender, of course, clamours for a surrender in return. Just as I have affirmed the other's being with my whole existence, so do I experience in his love the affirmation in return of my own being. The only person who knows himself surely and for certain, is the man who has had experience of himself as a centre towards which moves another's love. "*Amor, ergo sum* – I am loved, therefore (and to that extent) I am." Our person begins where it loses itself in another person.

Our *knowing* is also subject to kenotic a dialectic. Though it is true that our acquisition of knowledge appears to be a taking into our possession of another being and as such produces the impression of an emptying of the other, it is in fact in its completion an emptying of oneself. The characteristic thing about knowledge in its taking possession of its object is its subjectivity, the fact that it can set itself up over against the objective world as an independent, unifying cognitive centre that accomplishes its act at a distance which is a fact of being. Knowledge means confrontation, and it is only this that creates the objectivity of the object. It would be a mistake to think that this subjectivity could be assured by the knower's drawing away from his object, and increasing the distance so much that he becomes completely immured in himself. The necessary condition for the growth of subjectivity is, on the contrary, a renunciation of all self-centredness and an opening up of the subject to the objective world. The greater this openness, the keener will be the view on reality and the more powerful the knowing subject.

The kenosis of human knowledge is even more apparent in the activity that follows on and perfects the act of knowing. The subject is incapable of positing himself if he is immured in himself. He must identify himself with the task to be performed, he must place his centre of gravity outside himself, employ and, indeed, use up his strength, and in sacrifices and renunciations without end form the world. That is the only way in which he can fully posit himself.

Finally, the kenotic dialectic is very obvious in the act of knowledge *par excellence*, the knowledge of a person. The deep-down centre of a person, that place where lies the foundation of his true reality, has a name: self-possession in freedom. Knowledge can never of itself reach this point, unless, of course, the other reveals himself freely and of his own will. This means that the truest reality of a person can only be known through his own self-statement, a thing which it is quite impossible to verify. One can, of course, verify a person's truthfulness, sincerity, objectivity, as well as a whole lot of other things about him, but not what he says about his interior life. Nevertheless, the unverifiable statement can be accepted in faith. The first condition for this is that love should create round the other's person a space of "interiority" into which he can transfer his interior life without having to venture forth into an uncongenial world. The second condition is the acceptance of what the other says. This can only be secured by an attitude of trust, which creates an affinity between the knower and the known, and can only be attained in an intimate concern for the personal interests of the other, i.e. in the love that creates affinity. So we see that in its highest function knowledge assumes the form and, therefore, the kenotic attitude, of love.

Liberty is the highest form of self-possession; but let it be noted at once that to be free is "to be one's own destiny". He alone is free who fulfils to the last end "what is written" in him. To have a destiny, to be one's own destiny accordingly means to be extraneous to oneself, no longer to possess oneself, to be at another's disposal.

How we understand in detail this matter of "disposal" depends on how we interpret the inner structure of the world complex of being and, consequently, of what happens in the world. In any case this disposal is certainly an extraneous thing even if it does belong to the inner, individual structure of our existence. That being so, it is precisely this extraneous thing *in* us to which we must adapt ourselves in complete liberty, in order that, accomplishing our inner necessity, we may be free, i.e. entirely "ourself". Our freedom, our complete self-possession, comes into being at the very point where we no longer belong to ourselves.

Sometimes, under the veil of our daily experiences, we are able to perceive with quite extraordinary clearness the ontological exigency there is for the uniting of freedom and necessity, for, on occasion, our human existence enters on a state of what we may call euphoria. All at once, without apparent cause, things become transparent, the inner tempests of existence die down, we feel an ineffable harmony, look out on our destiny in all tranquillity and clarity, and accept it as a gift. In such moments of noonday brightness, in the light of what Paul Valéry calls *midi le juste*, our existence is seen by us to be irreplaceable and necessary in its inner pattern. At the same time we feel our free, untrammelled uniqueness: as a free decision I carry myself on towards my accomplishment. Hölderlin's German landscapes bathe in this light of the cosmic perfection of our free necessity. The highest form of liberty seems to be attained in an identification on our part with the necessity of our destiny.

Now, if death is total destruction, it follows from the general logic of kenosis that it must also be the possibility for total accomplishment in perfection. The complete positing of the self can only be effected in a complete destruction. But in that case our existence does not come completely to itself until death, and is only then posited as complete consciousness, complete knowledge, complete liberty and—dependent on this last—as complete love or complete hate. Thus the kenotically determined and limited acts of our existence point to the fact that in them man places himself in death by anticipation. The kenotic element in our existence is a previous sampling of death, a sampling of our total self-perfection in our total destruction.

8. *Revised Definition of the Whole Concept of the Process of Death*

Our philosophical meditation on death could well go further. We have developed the analysis of our immersion in death in the domains of volition, knowing, perception, remembrance, love, the historical dialectic of existence, poetic experience, and the kenotic act of existence. A similar demonstration could be made for other mental activities also. The exact analysis of artistic creativity,[31] of liberty as cause of being,[32] of the elemental experiences of sorrow, dissatisfaction, joy, anxiety, etc., would show how in these occurrences too man plunges himself into death, and show to what a great extent he, by anticipation, realizes death in them as a fully personal act. This would be a task as important as it is tempting. However, I hope I have already given all the essentials, and that the philosophical side of our hypothesis of a final decision will now seem to have been sufficiently argued and established. To conclude I should, however, like to point out some important results that follow from the analyses already made.

Right at the beginning, in the methodological investigations, I indicated that the classical *definition of the process of death* (the separation of the soul from the body) was unsatisfactory.[33] It immediately gives the impression that the destruction involved in death affects nothing but the corporal element which, detached from the soul and left to itself, must necessarily decay while the soul flies off almost unaffected. The analyses here offered to the reader's attention have already demonstrated in their various ways that death affects the soul itself, and inwardly. Destruction is an interior fact for the soul itself, in death. In death the soul is ontologically exposed to real and effective annihilation. At the same time, however, we must maintain that spirit by its very nature can never fall back into nothingness. In the moment of death there occurs an inner annihilation of the soul, but this is not capable of annihilating the soul's spiritual reality. The destruction of an indestructible—this is the contradiction our analyses would seem to have left us with.

We must now try to indicate the solution of this contradiction with the help of Thomist metaphysics. Aquinas tirelessly emphasizes the fact that man consists of one single essence in which matter and spirit are the substantially united principles of one single whole. Man is not a composition of two things. For Thomism the whole body and the whole of its activity are the work and activity of the soul. The soul is the form of the body right down to its finest fibres and minutest stirrings. On the other hand, the corporeal principle penetrates the spiritual so intimately that it belongs to the inner perfection of the soul. Body and soul are so completely one that in this one their duality actually disappears. Out of the two there comes a third which is neither of the two. The substance "man" is not a union of two substances, but a compound substance owing its substantiality to only one of its constitutive principles, i.e. the soul, as the *unica forma et actualitas materiae primae*. St Thomas thinks of the body as the unfolding of the soul. Our body, considered in all its dimensions, is, as far as its powers of expression are concerned, a still imperfect self-expression of the soul—only in the risen body does our corporeity attain its full spiritualization—for the simple reason that the soul is immediately present and active in the body as in the principle which is still engaged in unfolding it (the soul).

This conception of the unity of the "body-soul" is founded, in St Thomas's view, on the frequently misunderstood theory of the unicity of the substantial form.[34] The corporeal principle is not attached to the soul by some "accidental" relation. Rather is it posited by an act which is of the essence of the soul, that is, an act which is not distinct in reality from the soul. Relation to corporeity is part and parcel of the essential constitution of the soul, so that the body is included in the actuality of the soul as the form of the body. This relation does not, as one might think, arise between two beings only after they have been fully constituted in their individual essences; it exercises a dominant function in them before any further determination at all and makes them to be what they are. It is a transcendental, basic relation permeating all the levels, determinations and relations of the soul. Everything that appears in the corporeity must be understood to be the development of what is contained in the soul *originaliter et quoddammodo implicite*.[35] The soul, in other words, produces the corporeity out of itself with an inner necessity which is precisely what makes it a soul. The corporeity is "given" immediately and originally with and in the soul's essence. That is why the separation of the soul from the body cannot be understood as a simple sundering of two existent beings. Death is rather the total destruction of one of them and, therefore, an event of immediate, inner import to the soul itself. It is not possible for the body to be separated from the soul without the soul's being thereby exposed to destruction.

If, then, the soul too as "form" is the scene of a real ruin or dying, it, nevertheless, as "subsistent form" remains indestructible, i.e. immortal. Its state of separation from corporeity is in the richest meaning of the term "unnatural".[36] Through death the soul finds itself transferred into a state of ontological indigence.

Building on this hint Karl Rahner develops an hypothesis that, however daring it may seem at first sight, does, when we look into it more carefully, throw not a little light on our problem. He takes up St Thomas's teaching on the relation of the soul to the body and carries it on further in the line of its logical implications. In strict Thomist theory there is contained in the soul a transcendental demand for a relationship with matter (transcendental meaning immediately "given" in the very essence of the soul). What, then, happens to this transcendental demand in death? Could it be that God through some special intervention satisfies the still-continuing ontological indigence for an actual relationship with matter in order that the soul may be kept away—artificially, one might think—from any contact with a body? There is no reason whatever why we should implicate God in the explanation of processes involving merely secondary causes, as long as there exists any possibility of our finding a strictly immanent basis for them. Therefore, leaving the first cause, God, out of the question in seeking for a satisfaction of the soul's ontological indigence for a relationship with matter, we may assume that the soul's liberation from the body in death signifies something more than a mere breaking-out through the prison-walls of matter. We may, on the contrary, suppose that thanks to the process of death the soul is given access to a more really essential proximity to matter.

If we now endeavour to determine more closely the manner of this proximity, we find in the first place that in death the soul, far from becoming "a-cosmic", enters upon a meta-empirical relationship with materiality and becomes in a sense it is difficult to define but which is no less real, "pan-cosmic". Naturally, this pancosmic relation of the soul to the world (which it always had, but to which it opened up fully only in death) must not be understood as a "substantial informing" of the whole world by the soul. It is worth noting that, according to St Thomas, there exists a relationship of spiritual substances to material being that operates *per modum alligationis cuiusdam* without any sort of "informing".[37] This sort of meta-empirical relationship would transpose the soul to a state in which its "nature" grows out of its own roots of "essence" and "being". This means that the soul would break out of the empirical spatio-temporal pattern and reach the place where there occurs the self-development of the world in essence and being. This place would be the domain where the forms which give causality to the dynamism of being as it presses out from the world centre into the spatio-temporal sphere, work towards their entelechy. In other words: the soul reaches the place where the whole world has its source, where it is brought together and grasped as one whole, as it were centrally connected and fastened, the place where from the beginning we always had our roots of being and essence.

This earthy, empirical world of ours is, as it were, nothing more than a corner of that essential cosmos from which the force for existence flows into our world just like so many individual drops present each one but for a moment of time; of that cosmos the contact with which snatches our world ever and again out of non-existence by means of a new, tiny basis in existence, exposing it in this way to the headlong current of the river of time. Seen in this way death appears as a descent into the centre of our mother earth, to the root unity of the world —there where all the connexions end in one knot, where all spatio-temporal things join together, burgeoning on one root—down to the furthest and deepest of all that is visible. Perhaps one might express this reality with the single word "heart".[38] In the metaphysical process of death the soul reaches the "heart of the universe", the "heart of the earth".[39] This is the place where it will have to make its complete and final decision.

If we want to express symbolically this double process—on the one hand, the destruction of the soul and, on the other, its entry into the heart of the cosmos—the image that immediately offers itself is that of birth. Here the child is, so to speak, thrust violently forth from the confines of its mother's womb and forced to leave its protecting, accustomed, familiar *milieu*. It is exposed and threatened with complete destruction. At the same time, however, there opens up before the child a wide new world, a new relationship, the world of light, colour, meaning, community (*Mitsein*) and love. Something similar happens to the soul in death. Violently it is taken out of the confines of the body and world it has known hitherto. Simultaneously it reaches a new and essential relationship with the world stretching out through all the length and breadth of the whole world's being. The destruction is, therefore, a fact for the soul in two ways: (1) it really does disappear in the sense of undergoing an annihilation, a violent removal from its body-and-worldliness as hitherto known; (2) it goes deep down into the roots of the world and in doing so receives a cosmic relation to existence, a total presence to the world.

Let us now relate these considerations to our earlier analyses. The picture of death we obtain is something like this: In death the soul finds the sum total of all that any single one of its acts had ever aimed at (this is death as total self-encounter), and at the same time finds its firm roots in the original basis of the world (death as total presence to the world). These two events do not occur without a reciprocal relation. If we are to take seriously the Thomist theory of the essential relativity of the soul to the body and draw from it its ultimate consequences, no complete self-realization of the soul is thinkable otherwise than through its identification of itself with a presence to the world. Both are mutually related as the formal and material aspects of one and the same process. The soul takes hold of itself through the pancosmos, and by so doing—since it produces its relation to the world freely and creatively—it reshapes this whole cosmos for itself, essentially.

If this is so, then the soul is of necessity confronted whole and entire with God (death as total encounter with God). God stands in the prolongation of the soul's dynamism, God who has ever been present to men as the end they were seeking. The original basis of the world is also by nature open to God and transparent to the basis of all things that are, i.e. to the Godhead. This means that total self-encounter and the total presence to the world it contains are simultaneously an encounter with God. This does not at all mean that this encounter with

God may be called the vision of God, since man experiences the presence of God in death only in the image of his own human dynamism and in the longing expectation of God he finds in the basis of the world—through a kind of transparency, one might say. Still it is more truly essential than all the encounters with God experienced during life, put together. In death man is brought face to face with everything he can possibly aspire to in the depths of his longing, everything he can possibly guess at in all his acts of knowing, everything he can possibly blindly strive for in all his acts of volition, everything, fundamentally, he can possibly embrace in his love.

At the same time and in the very act of realizing the dynamism of his essential being, man is transported to the place where the whole of creation awaits God. In all this, in the striving of his own humanity and in the great press of the cosmos, he finds himself set face to face with the Lord of the world. At this metaphysical centre he is to make his final decision. The decision made here lasts for all eternity, for the excellent reason that this decision is not made under the conditions of our present provisional state with its multiple preoccupations and merely relative, conflicting truths, and not made in the midst of the dualism of this existence. (These conditions, inevitable in our earthly life, made it permissible for us to go back on our decisions, because these had never become "being" completely; they were never more than just "acts".) Now, however, act becomes being, decision becomes state, time becomes eternity. Death as complete self-encounter, as descent into the depths of the world, as ascent into the presence of God and as the entry—at last become possible—into a fully personal relationship with God by means of a completely free decision—these are the essential elements that constitute our hypothesis.

These insights into human death indicate a trend of thought that can be taken up and profitably explored by a line of theological speculation. We may suppose that these thoughts will disclose their full significance only when explored theologically. So that the philosophical foundation we have laid invites us naturally to theological meditation, and to this I propose to devote a special chapter of this work.

9. *Summary of the Philosophical Demonstration*

We have put forward seven arguments as a philosophical foundation for our hypothesis of a final decision.

Firstly, we used Blondel's *analysis of volition*. In our volition there is to be found on the part of the volitional drive an unreflective pursuit of an end, always going further than the concrete, actual realization of the will, the individual act of the will. This volitional drive is something imposed on us as pure necessity. In every one of its strivings it aims with all the force of its reality at taking up a position *vis-à-vis* God. This means that in every striving of the will we find as its innermost dynamism an unconscious *ecstasis* towards God. The conscious activity of the will, on the other hand, remains far behind this unconscious stretching out ever further ahead, and is incapable of catching up until it does so in death. So death is the birth of volition.

Secondly, we brought forward Maréchal's *analysis of knowing*. Like Blondel for volition, Maréchal discovers in knowing a fundamental dualism. As knowing subjects we live in a continual *excessus* towards God, unconsciously and unsystematically accompanying every act of judgement we make. This basic tension makes possible the actual knowledge of particular, earthly and sensible things. These two factors of human knowledge are reciprocally ordained one to the other. The only possibility for their complete mutual confrontation would be a coming to itself of the human mind, but the way towards a total self-reflexion is blocked by the material principle, for this is not as yet transfigured by the spirit. So it follows that the first integral act of knowledge, the meeting of the two lines of knowledge in a single act of total reflexion can be realized only at the moment of death when the spirit frees itself from material concretion not yet transparent to the spirit. In this act it forms for itself a new concretion, this time completely transfigured by the spirit.

Thirdly, we dealt with Bergson's *analysis of perception and remembrance.* Bergson established that the living being's mastery of the world is limited by the selective activity of perception. This operates as a sort of protective measure on the part of the mind and represents an essential condition for our mastery over the events of our day-to-day life. At certain moments of liberation we are made aware of an unsuspected widening of our field of perception.

Much the same is true of our remembrance. Our practical outlook on the world, our urge to get the future into our hands, both cause the past to disappear. Nevertheless, the moments of real relaxation enable the past to come to life again. Whatever the moments of relaxation and liberation that may occur during life, they are only pale reflexions of the real relaxation and liberation we experience in death. Accordingly death is the place of total intuition, i.e. of total perception and complete remembrance, the place of presence to the world and to life as a whole.

Fourthly, we followed out Marcel's *analysis of love.*

Our existence becomes being only in love. At the same time it is not possible for us to posit love in its essential reality. This is because of a self-seeking of our existence that leaves nothing untouched. Our first possibility of acting out our love fully is given us in the moment of death when our whole existence is exposed and surrendered. This ontological exposure (death) gives us the space we need for a decision of self-surrender (love).

Fifthly, we turned to the *dialectic of existence demonstrated in the history of the individual.* The first curve of existence, the "outer man's", plots the phases of origin, growth, development, progressive differentiation, withering, decline and, finally, decease. The second curve, opposed to the first, shows up the possibilities of ascent open to the "inner man". The creation of an independent centre of being, the widening of one's sphere of existence and the positing of one's own liberty, such are the possibilities offered us of this development. In the process, the energies of the "outer man" are transformed into person, but the highest and most decisive transformation can take place only at the point where these two curves cut, and that is death.

Sixthly, we dealt with *poetic experience.* Poetry is the founding of a new relationship with the world, and as such it constitutes the condition for an essential proximity to the world. Further, however, it is the positing of a complete isolation, supposing an essential remoteness from the world. At the point where the isolation becomes completely unconditional, the proximity to the world becomes so too. Death is, therefore, the place of our total presence to the world. Finally, since poetry is the summoning to us of the transcendent, this presence to the world is realized in a total encounter with God.

Seventhly, we mentioned the *kenotic actualization of*

existence. The basic functions of existence: consciousness, love, knowledge and liberty, all go through a like cycle of being, non-being and being again. Starting from an initial content of being, existence, with a gesture of self-abandonment, proceeds to the negation of that same content of being and by this path reaches a new fullness of being. Through destruction we reach being. So death must be understood as perfection in destruction.

In a final consideration we then undertook a revision of the *definition of the process of death.* Death is not only the destruction of the body; it is also a destruction of the soul in so far as it is realized in a material concretion. This destruction is an annihilation, reaching right into the centre of the soul, its body-and-worldliness as hitherto known, and also a descent into and immersion in total presence to the world. In this process the soul's new pancosmic relation must be regarded as the material element in the complete self-accomplishment of existence. The essential dynamism of the human estate and of the cosmos experienced in this way form together a *signum,* a transparence on God's part, and as such make possible the total final decision in death.

All these indications taken together give us the picture of death which we outlined originally in our hypothesis of a final decision: *Death is a man's first completely personal act, and is, therefore, by reason of its very being, the place above all others for the awakening of consciousness, for freedom, for the encounter with God, for the final decision about eternal destiny.*

III

THEOLOGICAL DISCUSSION

III

THEOLOGICAL DISCUSSION

THE RESULT of our philosophical reflexions was that the process of death shows a double structure: the formal side—a total self-encounter, and the material side—a universal presence to the world. These, however, are merely facets of one and the same reality. Existence is completely immersed in the cosmos *because* it becomes completely present to itself. And then, because God himself stands at the point where the expectations of the cosmos meet and the dynamisms of human nature come together, the twofold conquest of existence—of its own self and of the universe—also signifies an *encounter with God.* Thanks to the essential sign given him in the basis of the world and thanks to the transparence of his own being, man, in the process of death, experiences God as the transcendent centre of significance in the dynamism of created being. On this insight philosophical reflexion slips easily into theological meditation.

Our entry into the domain of theology entails a change in perspective and, by the same token, a redrafting of our method. In this section I intend to remain faithful to the *method of theological investigation recommended by the First Vatican Council.* It consists in the understanding of an object of theological research on the basis of "the connexions of the mysteries with one another".[40] That is to say, if an hypothesis throws light on various articles of faith, if through this hypothesis the individual truths gain in homogeneity, if finally, with the help of this hypothesis, the dogmatic data so often treated in a separate or even disparate manner can be brought together in a more unified view, then one may legitimately assume that it points to some truth already present in the content of faith.

That is why the only value the following considerations can possibly have is as a *theological essay*, an experiment carried out with one single basic thought: an hypothesis elaborated in another domain is imported right into the centre of a theological complex of relations in order that we may see whether this hypothesis will enable us to form a more unified thought-pattern affecting them all. The hypothesis of a final decision as suggested in philosophical terms is now to be applied to very finely interconnected theological problems. We shall then see what it is capable of doing for us. Though it is, of course, a delicate method, it seems to me to be the only one capable of breaking new ground for our speculative theology.

1. *The Ending of our State of Pilgrimage*

For our first point of contact we take the doctrine of the *inalterability of the state we reach through death.* A human existence that has passed through death has reached a final state in which no further change is possible in its basic tendency. At death a man's final figure with the destiny it deserves is irrevocably attributed to him. Once beyond death no more decisions altering the course of one's existence can be made. Death makes human decision irrevocable. One's decision as regards God now becomes final, permanent, unchangeable being. "In the place where the tree falleth, there it shall be."

The finality of this state obtains not only in the reprobate—those who have turned away from God and can no more come back to him—and in the blessed—those who are turned towards God and can no more abandon him—but also in those who are destined to the place of purification, for their movement towards God can no more be diverted and turned aside. Death, therefore, is the dawn of finality. In it man receives his definite shape. Death transports existence to the realm of things "valid for eternity", to the state of the "done once and for all". Out of human death there grows a fundamentally new dimension of existence—the finality as of the closed file, the definitely, irrevocably settled matter. *But how can we account for this finality?* The decisions of our experience never possess the quality of inalterability; on the contrary, they are characterized by an essential temporariness and a fundamental liability to revision. They never penetrate so deeply into our existence that they could possibly become being, and a state of finality. If they could, any thought of conversion, of dissociating oneself from one's own decisions would be impossible. What is it then in death that, all at once, closes off our open end of *fieri*? What transfers our human liberty into the dimension of completion? In these questions, we are enunciating one of the most complicated and thorny of all theological questions. It would be no small achievement for the hypothesis of a final decision if it could manage to throw a little light on this problem.

The question then is: How are we to account for the inalterability of human existence after death? The immediate answer is: The finality of the last state is due to the fact that God has willed that at death man's time of probation should end. But this is nothing but a statement of *what* happens, not of *why* it happens. Certainly God wills that man's time of probation should end at his death. That is not the question at issue. Should we not ask further: *But why does it end then?* How does God effect this termination of the temporariness and reversibility of our human decisions? After all, the soul loses none of its spirituality in death, and, in consequence, neither does it lose any of its freedom. What then prevents it from continuing to exercise its liberty of choice and to revise its earlier decisions? To this one often hears the deceptively simple answer: The finality of man's state after death must be attributed to a special intervention on God's part, which we must understand to be an essential element in the so-called particular judgement when God finally fixes a man's eternal destiny. In this view we should need a *special intervention of God* to prevent any further free acts capable of altering the course of an existence. But if God transposes human liberty into the state of lasting finality only by putting it into cold storage—if we may so express it—and prevents, from outside, any further changes of course, then this final state of man, whether it be eternal bliss or eternal damnation, is nothing but a mechanical superstructure lacking all personal depth and not penetrating beneath the surface of man's reality. Apart from that, the scientific principle of economy forbids our having recourse to a fresh intervention from outside, until we have exhausted every possibility of finding an explanation in the problem itself.

Moreover, God's transcendent—and transcendental—causality prohibits our looking to a special causal intervention of God for the explanation of the final permanence of man's state as reached in death. God endows us with the power of constituting by ourselves our own state of being out of our own resources. When God wills to obtain some end with any of his creatures, he does so in such a way that the end to be obtained comes forth "naturally", out of the resources immanent in the creature itself. Surely this is God's real greatness that he can so endow the creature as to make it its own causality without thereby limiting in the least his own all-operative and all-creative transcendent causality.[41] If, therefore, God's transcendent causality is to be preserved here too in the case of man's definitive entry into finality; in other words, if the fixation for all eternity of a man's decision is not to be understood as a special causal intervention or as an eternal prohibition and a structure imposed on the soul from outside by God—then we must look for some *inner factor in our creatureliness* itself which can give rise to the constituting of our human being in its ultimate finality.

When God wills a thing, his will always has an immanent *terminus* in its object. This is the direction in which St Thomas looked for a solution: "As there is in bodies a weight or lightness by which they are borne towards their place, which is the goal of their movement, so also there are in souls merits and demerits by means of which they reach their reward or punishment, which are the end of their activity. Therefore, as the body through its weight or lightness immediately finds its place, . . . so souls, immediately the bonds of the flesh are loosed—the bonds that restrained them during their state in this life—receive reward or punishment. . . . And because souls are appointed to their places in accordance with the measure of their reward or punishment, the soul, immediately on its separation from the body, is either thrust down into hell or else rises up to heaven."[42] This text, disembarrassed of course of its Aristotelian and mechanical terminology and examined for its deeper meaning, is of decisive importance for our question. It states that there is something immanent in man that settles the manner of his entry into finality like a court of his own being judging its own self, and lifting the moral value of his actions from within up into an eternal order. What is this immanent ground of the final determination of our existence?

Catholic theology has made various attempts to find this ground of final determination indwelling in our existence. The most important speculative *schema* consists in the *demonstration of the immanent appetite for being* of the human will. In volition we find a natural inclination orientated towards value and value only. Freedom, therefore, can repose on one thing only: a cleavage in the experience of value. In only one circumstance can our volition be attracted to or repelled by an object, viz. when the object presents aspects of value and anti-value. Wheresoever a goal of limited value is presented to man's will, he is able to be free, i.e. to determine himself to act in one way or another, for or against the object. In saying that, however, we are also saying that where the will can see in an object nothing but value, it *must* adhere to that object. This adhesion to an object of unmixed value is not a lack of freedom. Rather on the other hand does it represent a freeing of the spirit from all enslavement to non-value and an unimpeded march towards self-fulfilment. To what extent can this theory throw light on our problem?

In the first place, it is incapable of explaining the eternal impenitence of the damned. After all, these do not adhere desperately to a value that appears to them free of any admixture of non-value. The fundamental torment of the damned consists—does it not?—in their recognition of the absolute value represented by the Godhead, and in their striving towards it with all the fibres of their appetite for being, at the same time as they reject it. This theory, therefore, cannot provide us with a basis which will explain why the damned can no longer alter the basic orientation of their volition, unless we once more have recourse to the earlier theory of a special intervention of God. But the ineptitude of this has just been demonstrated.

For this matter of eternal impenitence we must delve still deeper into the immanent grounds of freedom to try to find some possible explanation. But even in the case of the inalterability of the state of the blessed, this theory appears on closer examination to be highly suspect, though it imagines it offers an incontrovertible interpretation inasmuch as the will of the blessed embraces God as pure and absolute value and, as such, adheres to him immovably.

One must, of course, retain unreservedly—and on this point we approve the basic position of the theory—that absolute value once fully realized makes impossible any further change in direction for our liberty precisely because of the will's appetite for being; further also, that the soul once entered into the vision of God adheres freely—and at the same time, necessarily—to the absolute value of God. But the question still remains how an absolute value can be realized in human volition at all. Does the essential orientation of one's freedom become inalterable because infinite value was presented to the will as its object, or is it not rather because the will affirmed in a subjective decision infinite, objectively proposed value? Expressed in another way: Does the cessation of all possibility of change of will occur in some automatic way through the encounter with absolute value, or in a personal way in an act of human liberty? This question calls for a closer elucidation.

In our decisions we see that in every act of volition the activity of the subject presupposes the open horizon of being in all its unconstraint. Always and everywhere our freedom is face to face with absolute value, not, it is true, in the *vis-à-vis* of an encounter, but in an implicit manner in all the other experiences of value. In this way our existence is immersed in the infinity of divine value and dimly, as it were with closed eyes, without the help of light, senses its plenitude in a speechless, inexpressible flowering forth towards its warmth. But why can our absolute opening up to infinite value not become an encounter with it? What prevents our existence from embracing its infinite fulfilment? The only possible reason is that our existence in its stage of multiple distractions is not in a position to throw the whole extent of its being into one single act of realization. That is why our realization of the infinite is never more than an expectant waiting for the infinite. The absolute always and everywhere "given" to us cannot "encounter" us, for the simple reason that we are incapable of taking up an absolute position in its regard. If our decision were absolute, i.e. if we could realize the whole range of our volition in one radical act of our liberty, then in this act we should behold absolute value in a veritable encounter. This encounter with the infinite thus presupposes as the condition of its possibility the *opening up of the concrete existence in a decision implemented through an act of absolute freedom.*

Have we not finally worked ourselves into a state of contradiction without issue? On the one hand, we maintained that *vis-à-vis* infinite value there is no decision, because the will is drawn towards it with the whole power of its immanent appetite for being. On the other hand, we were forced to recognize that the meeting with the embodiment of absolute value supposes a radical decision so far not realized. Is this not indeed a contradiction? Not in the least. After the encounter with infinite value has been realized, no further change of direction takes place in our freedom, but the encounter itself must take place in a free decision. Infinite value does not become absolute for us until the moment when we take up and make absolute our position in its regard. Even the blessed soul can adhere to God unswervingly only from the moment when it has taken its decision for God throwing into this act the whole range of its liberty. *The final determining* of its state has its ground, therefore, in freedom itself and is in the nature of a *decision.* The actual *final determination* of its state, its inalterable adhesion to the embodiment of absolute value embraced in a total decision, is, on the other hand, dependent on the will's immanent appetite for being. Volition encounters the absolute for the first time in its absolute act, in a total decision. For this reason the transition to finality can be understood only as a total, all-embracing decision.

At this point we can test the whole statement of the problem against the hypothesis of a final decision. If we assume that in death the human soul makes its decision for or against God in the full possession of its faculties, in complete lucidity and freedom, we shall be able to conceive the *final determining of the state after death as having the character of a decision.* In the context of the hypothesis of a final decision the essential thing about the process of death is precisely the fact that our existence, in one single act, is brought face to face with everything that until that moment it had performed through its dynamism of being in a merely unconscious and implicit way. In death it becomes possible for us to posit something absolute by way of our decision, i.e. to open ourselves up to the absolute. Since, however, a decision like this realizes once and for all the whole extent of man's essential dynamism, completely transforming it into being, existence with this unhampered decision reaches the state in which all its possibilities of decision in regard to its last end are exhausted, and this is the domain of ultimate finality.

St Thomas Aquinas demonstrated very clearly this structure of final determination in the decision of the angels concerning God. In the angels' decision there could be no question of obscurity, conflicting claims, inexactitude of focus owing to instincts, clouding of vision by passions. The angels made their decision in total lucidity, calmly and coldbloodedly, one might almost say, and putting the whole of their being into the decision. Their being became decision and their decision being. So their eternal state was a product of the interiority of free decision, a projection, that is, into a duration without end of their independent responsibility as persons. According to the hypothesis of a final decision, the same thing would happen in man. St Thomas expressed the parallelism between the angels' decision and man's death in the famous sentence of St John of Damascus he is for ever quoting at decisive places in his works: "What the fall was for the angels, that death is for men."[43] The positing of a straightforwardly binding, irreversible decision is so completely connatural to the most intimate aspirations of human liberty even in its decisions before death, that the whole movement of liberty is only possible because in it is anticipated a last, final *prise de position* in regard to absolute value.

In the most insignificant acts of a man's liberty a

primal will is at work which, in spite of the trivial and passing nature of the thing actually willed, is really aiming at a freely chosen and inalterable finality. We have already dealt with this in our philosophical section dealing with the projection of volition into death.[44] Here we shall merely attempt a counter-check.

Let us imagine seriously that we should never have to die. The conviction that we were not doomed to die would be equivalent to a condemnation of our present freedom to senselessness, emptiness and indifference, and that would rob life of all its charm. (Let it be clearly understood that we are talking of our freedom as it is, deeply marked by history. We are dealing neither with man's freedom before the Fall, nor with Christ's freedom.) An unending life in a state of permanently enduring temporariness and incompletion would utterly cripple our freedom. Why undertake anything at all if we shall never come to the end of the time we have at our disposal? Why make plans, why exert ourselves, indeed why do anything at all? A life of endless possibilities would be nothing but a lazy monotony of boredom and indifference. Unlimited time would mean time exhausted and wasted before it even began! If we knew that man could never die, we should go mad.[45]

It seems we must envisage the problem of death from this negative point of view at least for a moment and allow ourselves to be influenced existentially by this experiment in thought. In it we discover the evidence of our inward striving towards a final decision. This counter-check shows beyond all question that our liberty must contain in itself the possibility of reaching that spiritual height where all inconstancy and reversibility are overcome in a free positing of ultimate finality. So then, the finality of the state reached in and through death is achieved in a decision, and is the mature fruit of liberty.

This theory of final determining leads us to a better understanding of the *nature of hell.* Often one hears as an explanation of hell that God rejects the man who turns from him, which is why the reprobate soul hates him eternally, though it does at the same time by the very necessity of its nature long for God irresistibly. Surely the solution to this problem suggested by the hypothesis of a final decision is less unworthy both of God and of man? God in his immutable nature becomes bliss for one and torment for another according as his love is accepted in deepest humility or rejected, in either case by a final, definitive decision. God calls all men to himself for all eternity with the same gesture of redeeming love. The only difference is that the same fire of divine love burns the one because he resists it, and in the other becomes everlasting light. The same love of God, calling and offering itself to both, is the eternal torment of the man who wills to damn himself, and the eternal fulfilment of the man who turns towards God. The same word of God is a single two-edged sword. If this is so, the damned soul hates God not because it has been eternally rejected by God, but because God's unchanging love, through the soul's own decision, has become unbearable to it.[46]

To explain in this way why and how a human act can become an inalterable state; to explain by what means a man can take on himself his total separation from God in such a way that for all eternity he will make no change in it, one must have recourse to the hypothesis of a final decision—so, at least, it seems to me. This hypothesis teaches us to view the ending of the time for temporary and alterable decisions as a factor arising out of the very stuff of human freedom itself, thus enabling us to reach a deeper, more unified understanding of the truth of faith that after death a man enters upon an eternal state.

In this connexion let us emphasize that the hypothesis of a final decision rightly understood does not in any way at all represent a *devaluation of the decisions made during life*, and gives no hold whatever to any sort of easy-going thoughtlessness, which, of course, one could only regret. The final decision is in part determined by the preparatory decisions taken during the course of a lifetime. It does, indeed, offer the possibility of correcting at the end all the decisions of a whole lifetime, but the complete re-directing of a whole life's fundamental orientation must always be looked on as an extreme case in the order of probability, a real one no doubt, but one which, because it is an extreme case, cannot be taken into account existentially. If we adopt Erich Przywara's terminology to express the whole thing, we may say that the final decision stands in a "relationship of in and above" (*eine "In-Über-Beziehung"*) with the preparatory directions taken during a whole lifetime. It grows out of them to exactly the same degree as it stands above them by giving its final, conclusive judgement on them.

It is an abuse of the hypothesis if it is used to diminish the import of human decisions, because, on the contrary, its whole object is to underline the importance of everything that enters into the category of decision. If ever it led anyone to adopt a reprehensibly irresponsible attitude, that would be the fault, not of the hypothesis, but of some particular presentation of it. The final decision is most intimately connected with the life that has preceded it. It is the fruit of the decisions that have prepared it, though it does stand above them by giving its final, conclusive judgement on them. If one—mistakenly—considers only its second function, the impression can arise in certain circumstances that the importance of all previous decisions is being diminished. If, on the contrary, it is clearly and unequivocally shown that the final decision is rehearsed, for good or ill, in every single act of a man's life; that even apparently insignificant human acts having very little indeed to do with any appearance of moral decision, inasmuch as they are intelligent acts, are preparing the final stand, then perhaps all the exhortations to repentance and conversion may acquire a new urgency, one they never had outside the hypothesis of a final decision.

Rehearsal for the final decision is the absolutely essential note of existence as being for death. This consideration makes it obvious why precisely the tiniest, most inconsiderable and inconsidered particular decisions of a lifetime, which taken together build up slowly a whole direction and pattern of life, are of importance for eternal life. This shows that the acceptance of the final-decision framework for one's life can produce a new sensitivity of conscience and cause us to exercise a vigilant watch over even the most trifling acts we perform. The hypothesis of a final decision is certainly not intended, as will become abundantly clear as our study progresses, to deceive men by leading them to imagine that the obligations put upon them for reaching heaven have now been reduced and the path thereto made easier. Moreover, it is quite ridiculous to assert that in the hypothesis of a final decision everyone would get to heaven, since no one could possibly be so perverse as to take a decision against God in full consciousness and knowledge of what he was doing. Does not Christ himself speak of legions of fallen angels? Yet their decision was precisely that. Here we see that our existential uncertainty of salvation and the need for watchfulness this entails, when they are seen in the perspective of the final decision, are rooted in something much deeper than a mere terror of being cut off at any moment by an unpredictable snip of the Fates' shears. That being so, unremitting watchfulness is not only not done away with; it is reinforced.

> Although the final decision occupies a privileged place among all our decisions, it does not diminish the importance of the single successive decisions of a lifetime, out of which, in a steadily increasing way, our final attitude is being built up. Every act of our life aims either at communion or at isolation. What then can give us the assurance that at the end we shall upset all this slowly constructed orientation? Therefore, the final decision too will depend on us. There is no other measure for the sincerity of my desire for conversion than this conversion itself, now, at this moment. If life is a training for conversion, as the hypothesis of a final decision never ceases to insist, then at every moment we must make the same sort of decisions as we would make in death. . . . How shall we change later, unless we begin now? Procrastination is an existential lie. What I should like to be in the future, I must begin to be in the present.[47]

2. *The Place of our fully Personal Encounter with Christ*

We find our second point of contact in the doctrine of *salvation as personal fellowship with Jesus Christ.* This consideration will develop the preceding one in a new direction. Christ is the sole Mediator between God and man. Salvation affects in the first place the human person, for considered in its basic aspect it is a process of divinization. That being so, there would seem to be no alternative but to see salvation as a personal fellowship with Jesus Christ.

The personal reality of the Lord or, as Scripture expresses it, his Name, is the only means whereby we can be saved. St Thomas recognized this personal element in our salvation in a most striking manner. For the salvation of any pagan born since Christ's coming he required a personal movement towards Christ, an explicit belief in the incarnate Son of God, as well as in the Trinity.[48] He showed himself much less exacting as concerns both belonging to the Church and the necessity for salvation of the sacraments, especially baptism. They are, of course, indispensable, but not in the same measure as the personal relationship with Jesus Christ. They cannot be replaced, but can be reached *implicite*.[49] This assertion of Thomas's only repeats what St Paul had insisted on, viz. that word and revelation are above institution and sacrament. The necessity of explicit faith seemed so indispensable to Aquinas that he was of opinion that a man who had never heard of Christ—and this eventuality, in the then state of geographical knowledge, must indeed have seemed an extreme though not impossible case, e.g. a man who, as St Thomas says had spent his whole life "*in silvis et inter bruta animalia* – in forests and amongst the brute beasts"—Aquinas thought that such a man would in case of need receive this knowledge in a particular, immediate, interior but still expressly perceived revelation.[50]

If we consider the fate of this theologoumenon in the course of history, we are left with the impression that the science of theology—or is it perhaps only individual theologians?—has slowly retreated before the force of reality. Many theologians would be ready to interpret this development as real progress in spite of the fact that it obviously represents the abandonment of something very important.

The first step was taken when it was noticed that since the birth of Christ the numbers of men living in "remote forests" who had never heard of Jesus Christ was to be reckoned not in tens but in hundreds of millions. In the light of this discovery St Thomas's teaching seemed altogether too hard and exacting. So the required minimum of explicit supernatural faith was reduced. The explicit faith in the incarnate Son of God and the Trinity became a belief in the existence of a personal God and an eternal retribution that would come from him. In this belief all the truths revealed by God were contained *implicite*. If the pagan, in addition to the charity (or contrition) necessary for justification, also possessed the intention of serving this God sincerely, this attitude would then include an implicit desire for baptism and membership of the Church.

When in the course of time it became only too obvious that vast numbers of pagans and paganized Christians could not possibly satisfy even these minimum requirements, that they had absolutely no idea, at any rate as far as the practical ordering of their lives was concerned, of any such personal God, theology once more retreated before the evidence of reality. A distinction, considered to be absolutely essential, was worked out between the "real belief" and the "formulation of this belief". It was said, for example, that a man was not always capable of giving adequate expression to his experience of the absolute. He might project the appetite for the absolute that is inherent in his existence on totally alien ideas, realities and institutions, which he would then embrace with religious devotion. In such an attitude there would be manifested, they argued, an inner conviction and belief in a personal God and just rewarder of right and wrong, no less real for not being conceptually elaborated and consciously formulated.

Theology's third retreat before the evidence of the facts was its talk of the unconscious longing for God that can give pattern and moral purpose to a life without any explicit knowledge on the part of the person concerned that this is in fact so. In this case it would be quite sufficient—so went the argument—if a man were to actualize in any way at all this longing for God given him with his existence itself. This complex of man's unconscious longing for God could indeed be actualized in places where we should never dream of looking for it. In an act of love for a fellow man, in the sacrifice of one's personal interests, in an experience of the nothingness of things and so forth might well be contained implicitly a formal act of belief in a personal God. Furthermore, it was pointed out that men can be found who, as far as religion and morality are concerned, are nothing more than infants, even though their other faculties have developed in an entirely normal way; and that the immersion of existence in a given social *milieu* reaches such depths that the primitive moral experiences stored in the conscience can, in actual fact, never come to the surface of consciousness. So we can have the case of a man whose life is completely amoral, who has no knowledge of God or even consciously rejects him, seeing in him, for example, a means of "capitalist exploitation", and who yet, in spite of all that, is well and truly on the way towards salvation, because his unconscious longing for God somewhere or other does manage to become a donation of his entire personality.

We have no intention here of contesting that that sort

of thing not only can occur, but indeed does occur. Moreover, it is certainly a very fine thing to want to assure the salvation of as many men as possible. Again, it is true that God's efficacious will that all men should be saved is everywhere present and can take hold of men in regions to which their consciousness never reaches. In this sense, the discovery of the above-mentioned points from which a man may reach out towards faith really does represent an important advance in theology. Nevertheless, that must never cause us to forget that a man is a man really and in the fullness of his personality only when he goes after some ideal in the clear consciousness and the liberty of his whole existence. So men cannot be saved by means of a logically impeccable minimalism. The Christian life is a life of grace; that means, a life of divinization, and divinization affects, primarily, the person in its spirituality. This means that it takes place in a domain of lucidity, decision, love, in a word, of personal values. One is not divinized without knowing about it explicitly; just as one is not rejected unless one has decided in complete lucidity that one wants to be. Gods cannot be manufactured; they can be formed out of men only through a personal relation to the God-Man in a being-with (in fellowship) with Jesus Christ.

Two basic demands are thus discovered tugging our theological effort in different directions. The realization that God's will for the salvation of all men is a universally efficacious will, compels the theologian to try and explain how everything, even the least personal and apparently senseless and insignificant things, can be the expression of this will for salvation that God has anchored in the depths of human existence. Over against this he sees the inescapable necessity of throwing into relief the role of the person of Christ in the work of salvation and likewise the need to situate the process of divinization in the domain of the person, in other words, to see salvation as consisting in the establishing of a personal relationship with Jesus Christ and the explicit adopting of a position as regards him.

The hypothesis of a final decision gives us a possibility of satisfying both demands. In it we can understand how the decision for or against Christ known by the person in perfect lucidity can be a possibility for all men without exception. Death as the final decision takes the whole weight of our existence and throws it, in an act which concentrates in one all the riches of our person, into one final choice for or against. On the other side, it is made equally obvious that the final decision is being prepared the whole time, growing out of the most trivial decisions right in the midst of the obscurities and conflicting claims of life. As a result we can approve the following statements: (1) salvation is achieved only in a formal and explicit movement of one's life directed towards Christ in faith; (2) salvation is prepared and, as it were, rehearsed by pagans—as well as by Christians—through the ordering of the acts of existence in the direction of death.

None of the theories of an implicit reaching out towards the Church and baptism loses anything of its relevance, quite the contrary. In the philosophical part of this work we have explained at length how even in its slightest stirrings the whole of existence tends towards the final decision it will make in death. These tendencies definitely make place for a great deal of "implication", so that the theories based on this idea of implication are really reinforced and enriched while, at the same time, they have their minimalism pruned away.[51] In this way the hypothesis of a final decision would appear to have gained in probability when viewed from this second theological angle.

3. *The Universality of the Redemption*

We find a third point of contact in the doctrine of the *universality of the Redemption.* From the general discussion of our problem developed in the preceding point a new question arises. We have seen that the hypothesis of a final decision offers all men without exception—not excluding the imbecile and mentally defective—the possibility of making in death a fully personal choice for or against God. This corresponds perfectly with the demands contained implicitly in God's will for the salvation of all men.

Christ died for all men without exception and through his death and resurrection has created a new and universal scheme of salvation in which the whole of mankind is polarized through the acceptance or refusal of Christ's offer of grace addressed to all men without exception. There is no half-way house in the scheme of redemption. Theologically this is an absolutely unassailable principle. Yet one question does still remain open: What happens to unbaptized infants who die before attaining the age of reason?

Some theologians, indeed the majority since Abelard (1079–1142), limit the proposition of the universality of the redemption by denying that it extends as such to unbaptized infants who have died without coming to the use of their mental and spiritual faculties. How do they come to impose this unexpected limitation? Their reasons can be summarized as follows.

Baptism, either of water or desire, is absolutely necessary to salvation. But the children in question are incapable of eliciting the mental act of desire for baptism. Therefore, they can be saved only by the baptism of water. The salient point in this argumentation is the assertion that children cannot be saved by the baptism of desire because they are incapable of any mental act. How can one be certain of this? If we can demonstrate that in their death children too awaken to the full possession of their mental and spiritual powers, the argument breaks down.

These theologians work on three clearly defined data: (1) the proposition affirming the universality of the redemption; (2) the principle of the impossibility of sharing in the redemption otherwise than by a free decision (this is equivalent to requiring baptism at least *in voto*); (3) the supposition that there are in fact unbaptized infants who die without eliciting any act of decision from their will. Since these three data are absolutely irreconcilable, and as these theologians are not prepared to consign these little creatures to hell like their rivals the so-called *tortores parvulorum*, they elaborate an hypothesis which enables them to hold all three data at the same time. This is the *limbo hypothesis*. "Limbo"—in Latin, *limbus*—originally means a border, hem or fringe, and was thought of as a place bordering on hell. Essentially limbo would form a part of hell and would, therefore, not be an intermediate place; its inmates, however, would not suffer the pains of hell. They would indeed be excluded for ever from the vision of God, but would not really have any consciousness of this exclusion, and would even enjoy a so-called "natural beatitude".

This line of thought can make no claim to the authority either of Scripture or of Tradition. It has never been adopted as the Church's dogmatic teaching. When, however, the Jansenists tried to have the defenders of the limbo hypothesis branded as heretics, the Church condemned the Jansenists. She really cannot accept that her scholars, engaged in serious research and attempting to save as many poor little creatures as possible, at any rate from the pains of hell, should be the objects of ecclesiastical censure on the part of fanatics eager to condemn as many as possible to eternal damnation. We see at work here a deep-lying intention of the Church: a preference for the "more lenient solution". The limbo hypothesis itself did not receive any greater degree of certainty through this measure. If we can find another hypothesis which, while showing the same leniency, can give us a better solution of the problem, there is nothing to prohibit our abandoning the limbo hypothesis.

For some time now the criticisms of the hypothesis of a *limbus parvulorum* have been multiplying on all sides.[52] This hypothesis appears to introduce into theology a concept full of contradictions which makes of it a most inappropriate cement for the joining of different data of faith. It is by no means clear how a man could be eternally separated from God and even enjoy a "natural beatitude" without suffering the pains of hell. Christ's redemption and God's will that all men should be saved—which it includes—produce ontological effects in the order of reality. One of these is the total ordering of each man in his concrete historical destiny towards his supernatural end; and this is a condition *a priori*, an ontological prerequisite for his existence as a spiritual essence. What then does a "natural beatitude" signify in this context? Theology, of course, does know the concept of *natura pura*, or, to be more precise, it forms this concept in order to be able to embrace in thought without contradiction God's twofold liberty in both creating man and elevating him to his supernatural dignity. That does not mean, though, that man as he is and has become in the course of his history, is not, with every ounce of his being supernaturally ordained to God as to his last end long before any stirring of his spirit takes place. Any reasonably penetrating analysis of our concrete spiritual dynamism shows that the area we call supernatural is something "given" and present in the *de facto* composition of the human being. Our historical existence is already so profoundly affected by the supernatural that it is simply impossible to extract the "natural" dynamism from our existence as it is, and display it in its "pure state". Through Christ's work of redemption there has been formed in man a permanent disposition not due to his nature as such and ordaining his whole existence towards a supernatural fulfilment, a disposition which provides the ontological basis for his activity as a person and is not merely the product of his free act as a person.[53] This efficacious and ontological ordering of man to his supernatural end which must, of course, be distinguished from the justifying possession of sanctifying grace, is one of the most real of all the facts of human existence. The task God lays on us is a call to our existence and a call that is creative of reality.

If that is true, how can one assert that a human creature whose whole being longs for God in all its parts could bear, without suffering, the situation of internal conflict that would be produced by an everlasting separation from God? Unless, of course, one were to maintain that limbo is a kind of incubator for human chrysalids destined never to awaken to their spirituality. That, however, would be an equivalent affirmation of the defeat of creation running dead counter to the very essence of what spirituality is.

If, on the other hand, a creature endowed with spirituality, attains after death to the consciousness called for by its nature, it will be absolutely incapable of excluding from the realm of its experience its state of separation and remoteness from God. Hell is estrangement from God experienced as a state of being. The other torments of hell only become intelligible inasmuch as they flow from this central pain. The separation from God determines a cleavage that penetrates right to the heart of man, and also an ontological state of hostility to the rest of the universe as it presses on towards Christ, the selfsame universe in which man himself is immersed by reason of his nature.

These three cleavages enable us to explain all the pains of hell grouped under the headings of *poena damni* (pain of loss) and *poena sensus* (pain of sense). It follows, therefore, that any idea of an eternal separation from God that did not necessarily include in its content all the sum of the pains of hell is quite unthinkable. Yet that is precisely what the advocates of the limbo hypothesis, as distinguished from those of the old Augustinian school, were trying to avoid.

If now we substitute the hypothesis of a final decision for the limbo hypothesis, the whole problem is solved immediately. The quite arbitrary assumption that there are human beings who during their earthly pilgrimage never had the possibility of making a decision for or against God and thus of receiving baptism at least *in voto*, is shown to have no object. The whole conceptual construction which produces limbo is needless. In the hypothesis of a final decision even infants would be able to make their decision in full liberty and knowledge at the moment of death.[54] It must not be forgotten that infants who die before they come to the use of their mental and spiritual faculties, are nevertheless creatures endowed with spirit, and they, like all other human beings, awake in death to their full liberty and complete knowledge. In death they too are brought face to face with the essential dynamism of their spirit and also with the basis of the world, and in this confrontation meet their Redeemer. The supernatural light that mysteriously surrounds the spirit of man and without which, if he is not to be destroyed in his very essence, he cannot be conceived as a concrete, historical existent thing, becomes in death a consciously perceived reality to children also, even quite apart from any "special illumination". At the same time they too are planted firmly in the basis of the world where the whole cosmos waits expectantly for God, in order to be received into the glory of the sons of God. Strictly speaking, if the word "infant" is to retain any meaning at all, we can no longer use it to describe a spirit which in death awakes to the fullness of its spirituality. We do not, after all, call the angels who were put to the test in the first moment of their existence "infants".

In death the infant enters into the full possession of its spirituality, i.e. into a state of adulthood that many adults themselves never reach during their lifetime. The result of this is that no one dies as an infant, though he may leave us in infancy. The decision of these "infants", if we consider its structure, must be very like that of the angels: their state of pilgrimage too was concentrated into one single moment and their decision developed at once into an eternal state.[55]

We must, of course, admit that the interpretation here proposed of the fate of unbaptized infants cannot claim for itself the authority of a long theological tradition. This, however, is no motive for rejecting a theological hypothesis. When Abelard proposed his limbo hypothesis, he could not take refuge in any really important tradition of the Schools either, in order to support his theory against the dominant theological ideas of his time. Compared with him, we have a considerable advantage in that we come after him, for in the limbo hypothesis we have the really decisive and successful challenge made to the zealots of damnation. Seen correctly the position is not one of our disqualifying the idea of limbo, but of developing it further along the lines of its original intuition. What it was really trying to say is freed of its faulty expression, maintained, and carried on still further.

4. *Problems of Original Sin*

In the preceding reflexions a particular question was everywhere present though unspoken. We must now deal with it *ex professo* as the fourth point in our confrontation with the hypothesis of a final decision. This is the doctrine of the *state of original sin*. It is impossible for us to deal with this extraordinarily complicated question in its full extent. We are going to consider it from one point of view only, a point of view deeply based in Christian tradition, however surprising it may appear at first sight: The collective state of mankind arising out of the Fall has a double significance in the scheme of salvation. On the one hand, it is a force weighing heavily on mankind; on the other, it is a first sign of God's redemptive lovingkindness.

Firstly: The first parents of the human race committed a grievous sin by transgressing the commandment destined to test their good will. They lost thereby sanctifying grace and incurred the pain of everlasting damnation (the first sin). They became subject to bodily death and the tyranny of the devil, and they suffered a change for the worse in both body and soul. Adam's sin —in spite of a radical change in the way the documents are understood, the majority of theologians continue to hold that Adam's sin alone, not that of both our first parents, was decisive—Adam's sin, as the sin of the first father and head of the human race designated by God, has descended to all his offspring and caused in them a "guilt" of a special kind. This is an interior, truly sinful constitution proper to every man, the absence of the God-given state of grace involving the loss of sanctifying grace, the lack of the supernatural gifts consequent on grace, the tyranny of concupiscence, death and suffering, the tyranny of the devil, the wounding of nature. The basis of the transmission of this sinful state (strictly, hereditary sin, but invariably called original sin) is the natural connexion through heredity with the father of the race. What follows must be understood against the background of this traditional teaching.

Secondly: There is an element intimately connected with and absolutely inseparable from the whole Christian interpretation of existence. The state of moral weakness in which we find ourselves as a result of original sin is, despite everything, an expression of God's will that we should be saved. For St Irenaeus (*c.* 130–*c.* 200) man's expulsion from paradise and from the state of original righteousness (justice) was not so much a punitive action on God's part as an act of compassionate loving-kindness. "It is for pity that God removed man far away from the tree of life, . . . for fear he might remain a sinner for ever and sin itself become immortal and evil unending and incurable. So he set a stop to transgression *by interposing death and putting an end to sin by causing the flesh to decay in the earth,* so that man might in the end cease to live for sin and in dying might begin to live for God."[56] The double significance in the scheme of salvation suggested in this passage is one of theology's most involved questions. In the ecstasy of joy Easter brings us it is easy enough to cry out: "*O felix culpa!*" It is a good deal more difficult to indicate theologically the exact structure of the gift of grace mysteriously contained in the very essence of our fallen state as it is caused by original sin. Irenaeus's understanding of original sin suggests that we look for evidence of God's gracious lovingkindness in the fact of the decomposition of the flesh. We now propose to attempt this—alas, far too briefly—as this will allow us to confront once again the hypothesis of a final decision and the problems of systematic theology.

Original sin and death are very closely linked. This statement presumably requires no further elucidation. In the biblical account of the Fall death is clearly understood to be a result of the loss of the grace of original innocence. The Bible attempts to provide an explanation for a whole series of perplexing facts of existence, and more especially the facts of suffering and death: "Of the tree of the knowledge of good and evil you shall not eat, for in the day that you eat of it you shall die."[57] This, however, was not a warning of instant death, for, according to the biblical account, our first parents went on living for a very long time after the Fall. The warning must, therefore, be understood as meaning: "If you sin, you will become subject to death", and, as a matter of fact, this is exactly what is expressed in the subsequent sentence of condemnation: "In the sweat of your face you shall eat bread till you return to the ground, for out of it you were taken; you are dust, and to dust you shall return."[58] What is decreed as the punishment of sin is not any kind of death, but the particular death which is a return to dust; that means a death of separation, disintegration, taking apart and stripping down. In pointing this out we have also—equivalently—put our finger on the precise nature of the immortality enjoyed in paradise.

Accordingly, we may assert that the praeternatural gift of immortality does not exclude death of every kind, but only *death as disintegration*. This view is strengthened by the Council of Carthage (418): "Anyone who says that Adam, the first man, was made mortal so that, whether he sinned or did not sin, he would die in the body, that is, would go out from his body not as a requital for his sin, but by a necessity of his nature: let him be anathema."[59] In his original state which, in the mind of the Council, includes the natural faculties as well as supernatural elevation and the praeternatural gifts—the internal logic of the whole state as combined out of these three elements is called the "necessity of nature"—man would, therefore, not have had to die "in the body". The Council did not say that man in his original state in grace would have been able to go on "living" indefinitely, and that he would, in other words, have been subject to no "death" at all. It merely said that his "death" would not have had the character of a "separation of the soul from the body". Karl Rahner describes the situation as follows:

> If death is the consequence of the fall of the first man, this implies that, before his sin, the first man was not subject to death. It is not legitimate, however, to infer from this proposition of faith that the first man in Paradise, had he not sinned, would have lived on endlessly in this life. Rather can it be said with certainty that he would surely have experienced an end to his life, but in another manner; maintaining the integrity of his bodily constitution, he would have conducted

> this life immanently to its perfect and full maturity. In other words, Adam could have brought his personal life to its perfect conclusion in its bodily form through a "death" which would have been a fact of pure, active self-engendering. He would have achieved a stage of perfection in which his bodily constitution would not have excluded that openness to the world in its totality which we now await as the final result of the redemption, and as the eschatological miracle of the resurrection of the body. This end of man in Paradise, a death without dying, would have been a pure, manifest and active consummation of the whole man by an inward movement, free of death in the proper sense, that is, without suffering any violent dissolution of his actual bodily constitution through a power from without.
>
> This insight is rich in meaning, not only in its reference to the fate of man in Paradise (now removed from all possibility of realization), but also in that it draws our attention to the fact that not every aspect of death can be considered a consequence of sin that ought not to have been.[60]

Seen in this way, Adam's non-subjection to death can be understood as the grace of non-disintegration of the body. The "death without death" of our first parents would have been something different from a handing over to decay. As a result it would not have included the aspect of dissolution, of stripping down to existential impotence, and of separation established between the living and the dead. It would have been simply the act of a man's existence attaining its final, definitive maturity. From his original state in grace man would have passed immediately into the state of being that is resurrection, without having had to abandon his body previously. This consummation would have been the effect of the holy vigour and abundant life of the human spirit raised through grace: spiritualization, transformation, transition. His perishable corporeity would have refashioned itself at the moment of "transformation", of "birth into eternal life", into a spiritualized bodily form. Therefore, when we speak of death as an effect of original sin, we must be careful to define exactly what we mean. Since the Fall and as a result of the Fall our transition into the full intensity of our true existence must be realized by means of a total separation. This *separation* is the distinguishing factor between Adam's non-subjection to death in paradise and our subjection to death here on earth since the commission of his sin. Now, if our state as creatures shorn of their powers through original sin is to be not only a punishment but also, as St Irenaeus suggests, a sign of God's gracious mercy, then this twofold character must be present and visible after some fashion or other in the separation of death.

In this way our general question has been narrowed down to the following particular problem: With what meaning of the words can the separation that is part and parcel of our death and comes to us through original sin be claimed as a sign of God's merciful lovingkindness and as an event in the scheme of salvation? If we call in the help of our hypothesis of a final decision we obtain the following answer: The separation in death is the very thing that gives all men a possibility of escaping from the existential environment of original sin and pushing through into the sphere of being where the state of original sin can be laid aside in a total decision for God. This statement calls for further clarification in two different directions: (1) What is the ontological constitution of the existential environment of original sin? (2) How does the separation of death make it possible to step out of this environment?

Firstly, let us deal with the question: *What is the ontological constitution of the existential environment of original sin?* The general résumé of the doctrine of original sin set out at the beginning of this section is an attempt to maintain simultaneously three points of dogma:

(*a*) In the scale of being, original sin is lodged at the level of the community. Through the simple fact of belonging to the human community, of being immersed in the whole series of its successive generations, of being descended from the God-appointed father and head of the human race, the individual is excluded from the justifying possession of sanctifying grace. "Original" sinfulness is, therefore, in the first place, something that reaches the individual existence from outside; from the sphere of the human community it insinuates itself into the individual existence.[61]

(*b*) This sinfulness that breaks into the individual existence from outside nevertheless becomes its own inner constitution. Through it man finds himself in an inner state of aversion from God. So that, although, in the scale of being, original sin is basically lodged at the level of the community, it nevertheless and just as basically becomes a constitutive component and an inner, essential belonging of each individual existence.

(*c*) This sinfulness breaking into the individual existence from outside and becoming there its inner constitution, cannot, however, simply take possession of everything in that existence. Within the concrete, individual existence it belongs to the "nature" as the *peccatum naturae*, i.e. to the realm of being present before any free self-"informing". It does not belong to the "person"—original sin is not a *peccatum personae*; that is, it does not belong to the self-positing of each individual which comes from his free act.[62] It is the situation which is always and essentially, antecedently "given" before every individual decision and within which a man is called upon to make his personal decision, to set his imprint on his existence and to come to an understanding of himself.[63]

Accordingly original sin has the following ontological structure, compounded of three elements: through the fact of his belonging to the series of human generations, a man finds himself living in an existential environment of sin antecedent to any individual decision on his part. Though this environment is exterior to him, it yet becomes the inner determination of his existence and excludes him from the justifying possession of sanctifying grace.

If we attempt to elucidate these three elements metaphysically and to sketch in the ontology contained implicitly in the doctrine of original sin but never examined and set out coherently according to its various stresses, we feel bound to turn to the world of concepts elaborated by recent philosophy in its rediscovered interest in everything concerning the person.[64] Fichte long since enunciated an idea that has since become axiomatic: "Only among men does man become a man."[65] Existence comes to itself in the *milieu* of being-with and being-together.[66] This structure of relationships with one's fellows has been brought right to the forefront of philosophical thought in the last thirty or forty years. Its fundamental concept of *being-with* has two closely related meanings which are, however, as concerns their formal content, radically different. Only the second of these is of interest to us here.

The first, more generally used meaning of "being-with" is the existential (*existentiell*)[67] one: the intimate involvement of men with one another which has its origin in the free creation of relationships.[68] The human person is not a finished dimension ready for use; it is an event. The person builds itself up in and out of its encounters. Out of its existence there rises up an urge to engage in communication with other existences. To begin with, this is a vague, almost imperceptible "movement outwards", but in the course of the encounters that actually occur, this basic movement gradually achieves coherence along certain lines. It makes for itself a centre of being and emerges to consciousness of itself. In this process there slowly appears what we may call the personal centre. It is only in encounter and in the freely chosen being with another, arising out of this encounter, that our existence grows into being a real person, i.e. into being *simpliciter*. The person as a free self-positing is not yet in being; it is non-existent until it is formed in a personal fellowship and communion, in the final analysis, in love. In the gift and as gift, we become a person, i.e. as the other's gift we begin "to be".

The second meaning of "being-with" is the "existentiary" (*existential*) one. From the very first moment of its existing, before any free defining of its position, any stirring of consciousness, the human existence is and exists from the other, from what it is not. From the start we are made out of the stuff of the other's being. The reality of our individual existence comes from outside ourselves. What is outside ourselves is, therefore, given and implicitly conveyed as the prime fact in every stirring of our consciousness. In this sense man is first and foremost what his previous relations with his fellows are. He is deeply immersed in a community which he had no possibility of choosing for himself. This community makes him, in his unadorned presence as what he is.

Only in the *milieu* of this being with one another that pours from outside into the individual existence, the *milieu* of being-with that essentially precedes any free setting of his personal imprint on himself, can man find the opportunity for a free decision.

Accordingly, it is not we ourselves who build up our existence. We come into being as the focus, we may say, of a movement pressing towards us from outside. What is outside ourselves belongs, therefore, to the innermost constitution of our existence with a double note: it is antecedent to any decision and it furnishes the basis for the possibility of the decision. Entirely built of the stuff of other people's being and planted in the strong, rich, fertile mother earth of the community—such is the interior and original constitution of existence. In the line of the metaphysical elucidation of the state of original sin a place of eminent importance must be ascribed to this existentiary being-with. For this reason we should like to show this more clearly with the help of two examples.

The fundamental place of existentiary being-with in the ontological structure of existence is demonstrated by an important discovery of modern anthropology. If we compare the new-born human baby with his nearest "relations" among the mammals, we are forced to recognize that the baby sees the light of day something like a year too soon! Not until a year after his actual entry into the world does the baby attain the degree of development a mammal of comparable class would have to attain at its birth. If this state of development were to appear in the human race after the fashion of a genuine mammal, the gestation period of the human female would have to be a year longer than it actually is. In this sense, then, we can rightly say that *man is biologically a premature birth.*

Comparing the development of human young with the more important traits of mammalian ontogenesis, we find that the most significant difference is that the new-born baby does not yet run true to the type of the mature specimen of the race either in mode of locomotion, stance or means of communication. Instead of remaining in the womb until he has reached a mature stage in his development, he is let out at a much earlier stage and brought into the world. Neither form nor behaviour is fully developed in the protection of the mother's womb in the case of the human animal. They are not fully completed according to the hereditary pattern of the race, nor do they come up to the requirements imposed by the *milieu* into which the baby is born. Man has to go through decisive phases of psychical and physical development outside the womb. Much earlier than any other mammal he is in the true sense of the word "exposed", thrown out into his future surroundings and all that that implies.

As he grows into these surroundings the characteristic peculiarities of his existence as a human being appear. Biologically he is a creature without means of existence, thrust out of the securities of contacts with an animal *milieu* and abandoned to himself without instincts by the side of life's highway. What is abundantly clear in this connexion is the fact that the actual "birth" of the child, i.e. his becoming an individual existence, happens in the bosom of the community quite some time after his arrival from his mother's womb.[69] This premature contact with his surrounding world of a creature provided with insufficient means signifies that man, by reason of his very nature, can be "delivered" only in a situation of relationships with the other men about him. Not until the so-called "extra-uterine spring" is over, is the human being really born, after sucking his fill, so to speak, of his surroundings. The psychic, educational, family and community influences, in a word, the whole gamut of influences received from one's fellow men belong to the essence of ontogenesis, to the development of the life-germ into a fully-developed, viable creature. Their role is certainly not merely to produce an imitative superstructure on an already fully constituted biophysical edifice.[70] All this makes it obvious that the community is anything but a merely extraneous adjunct to existence. On the contrary, it is a part, an essential factor, of existence itself. "Being" and "with" are the two ontological components of existence. They can be discerned in all it does, and mutually inform each other. Only in this knitting together in being of "being" and "with" do we find arising the concrete human reality "being-with".

Our concern here is not to enumerate in order all the vital points of existentiary being-with. With our second example we should simply like to point out a further insight which we are probably right in considering as one of the most important discoveries made by philosophy in our day.

From the beginning, the individual is inserted into a community of thoughts, feelings, values and options. This community is characteristic of the group into which he has been born. A mental and spiritual atmosphere surrounds the individual existence, an atmosphere in which it moves naturally and without question, breathing in its air hourly and daily. Hegel called this reality, common to all and, indeed, creative of the particular community, by the name of the *objective spirit*, because it forms the basic stratum of existence independent of the subject, as it were. Hegel may not have been the first to see the reality of the objective spirit, but he was certainly the man who penetrated most deeply into its structure. He was so fascinated by his discovery that he held the objective spirit to be the only historical reality. In the Hegelian conception individuals are nothing but imperfect dependent coinings minted by the objective spirit, entirely borne by it and never existent outside it.

N. Hartmann was largely successful in eliminating the too one-sided presentation of the original intuition. His research gives us, as far as its basic insights are concerned, an absolutely faultless interpretation of the objective spirit.[71] The effects of the objective spirit extend into all the spheres of life. It is active in us in its own way. Anything that is in harmony with it is accepted almost without resistance and, as it were, without our requiring any proof. What is opposed to the objective spirit can only with the greatest difficulty prevail against it. Its power seems to be well-nigh unlimited in the life of the individual. Starting with the first stirrings of life it moulds the existence of the individual, carries it along on its current, prepares its future and destiny. It does not merely stand outside the individual existence; it is active *in* it as the most intimate ground of the self. Its influence can be seized on by the individual only with considerable difficulty and even then usually in the encounter with persons who belong to other communities.

The objective spirit implants itself in the consciousness of the individual under the most varied disguises: language, accumulated experience and knowledge of the community, modes of behaviour, prejudices and basic attitudes. It actively forms its members, influences them, determines their personal self-understanding, their freedom, their attitude and to a large extent plots out the direction in which their activity turns. This spirit is not only the life-promoting atmosphere of each individual; it is also his great calamity. Often it succeeds in oppressing, disfiguring or seducing the personal spirit. It may even happen that false insights receive from it a kind of spurious, superficial perspicuity. It can enslave the individual existence, persecute it, oppose it without imagination or understanding and even take up arms against it in open warfare. By means of imperceptible influences it binds individuals together and brings them into dependence on itself. So then, it stands impersonally above its members but is active in them as a basic component of their existence, of their being-with. It is indispensable to the achievement of the individual existence and is the basis, the basic condition for every stirring of existence, inasmuch as it is antecedent to its every decision. It is one of the essential components of the complex of existence that we call existentiary being-with.

If we now ask how the single first sin of Adam is propagated; how, that is, it becomes in each descendant of our first parents his own inherited sin, a possible answer would be: *through the intermediary of a sinful existentiary being-with.* As a matter of fact, the explanation of the propagation of original sin through our sinful existentiary being-with would enable us to embrace in a single unbroken perspective the various basic factors operative in our state of original sin. It would become apparent why original sin is a state external to the individual existence, how it none the less becomes the innermost constitution of existence, and in what way it is always there antecedent to any personal decision.

The three factors operative in the structure of original sin: essential exteriority, constitutive interiority and pre-existence to any personal decision, from the combination of which is produced an ontological situation of estrangement from God, are, at the same time, determinations of existentiary being-with. Born into a community in which personal sin is rife as a dominant power, man assumes into his interiority these personal sins in their totality.[72] They become a constitutive content of his existence. He fills himself full of the sinfulness of the community—what the Bible in its understanding of existence calls "the world". Without any special punitive action on God's part, by the simple fact of his situation in the whole succession of generations, of his membership of a sinful community, man finds himself ontologically in an actual state of estrangement from God, and that means, outside the scope of sanctifying grace—all without any personal guilt of his own. This state of belonging to a world of sinfulness which breaks into existence from outside remains, of course, within the structure of existence, as being on the level of being-with antecedent to any decision.

Our effort to understand the traditional teaching on original sin leads us to the following description of the individual's "state of original sin". The state of original sin which has become part and parcel of the individual is his existentiary being-with with the totality of sinful mankind. The actual, personal sins of mankind become the constitutive content of the individual existence through the intermediary of his existentiary being-with. Adam's first sin is constantly being re-enacted in the sinful human community. It is detailed out in all the different personal sins of mankind. At the focal point of mankind's sinfulness there now arises an existentiary being-with branded with the mark of sin in each individual. In this way Adam's first sin is transformed into individual original, i.e. hereditary, sin.[73]

This view is confirmed by a consideration of the practice of the Church in baptizing infants. The deliverance of the child from original sin begins by his being presented with a new existentiary being-with which is not a sinful one. In baptism the child is adopted into a community in which the formative power at work is the grace of Christ. This grace breaks through from outside into each individual existence and in it becomes its own constitutive state of grace.[74] If original sinfulness is brought into the way of salvation through the presenting to each person of an "existentiary being-with of grace", then we must classify original sin itself in the category of being-with, as "sinful existentiary being-with".

After this rapid outline of the structure, we are now in a position to answer the second question we asked a little earlier: *How does the character of death as separation make it possible to escape from this existential environment of original sin?* The answer is: Through the total personalization of existence and through the possibility of a completely personal decision this contains. The ontological condition for the penetration of original sin into the individual existence in the way we have just suggested, and for its taking up its quarters in man's interiority, is the fact that man lives in a state of metaphysical disunion. In conformity with its actual ontological structure our human destiny works itself out on two different planes: (1) on the level of what can never be fully taken hold of, reshaped and marked by free decision, in other words, on the level of what is already there and is by its very essence antecedent to all that is personal; but secondly also, (2) in the realm of what is personal. In every free act, indeed in every spiritual act, the person experiences the impenetrability, the density and the active resistance of the nature that is its. It can never disappear without remainder in its acts, be they good or bad. The person can never achieve complete identification with its nature. It is incapable of spiritually transforming what is antecedent to the free act and antecedent as a condition of its very possibility, incapable of embracing in a single act of self-determination the whole expanse of human reality. So man is never a concentrated interiority. On the contrary, he is so very much delivered up to the outside world that elements extraneous to him can invade him and there become his inner constitution. This ontological structure is called in theological language, "concupiscence". This is the metaphysical determination of a creature that is exposed to existentiary being-with and, by the same token, to original sin.[75]

What now happens to this state of disunion in death? In the hypothesis of a final decision, man in the act of death achieves complete identification with himself, with nothing left outside or over. *He reaches in the order of being a state of "no remainder"*: what is personal in his essence can exercise itself to the full and dispose of the whole of existence either for or against God. The whole human reality carried along on the flood tide of what is personal enters into this decision. The nature of the man concerned is completely marked, impregnated; and in his existence nothing remains that has not been assimilated into this total self-understanding. Accordingly, man in death enters a sphere of being into which no disunion can follow him. The man now concentrates himself fully as a person, and is no more distracted by what is outside, what is antecedent to his decision, by the world. In death existence reaches that total intensity and centrality of the fact of being a person that makes possible the complete concentrating of all the man's forces without exception into his decision. This then separates him at one stroke from all that had been antecedent to this decision. So, in this way, man's metaphysical dissipation is done away with, and consequently any sort or trace of existentiary being-with is finally extruded from his existence. But this means that, at the same time, his state of original sin is abolished. How does this happen?

This question is posed in the most radical possible manner in the hypothesis of a man's dying still with the traces of uneffaced original sin. This man is now completely centred, as we have just shown, on his being a person. But what does this mean for his original sin? By becoming completely itself in death his person becomes open to God; this man is now able to decide about his whole existence in God's sight.

If he makes a negative decision, he sets himself up, with the whole fullness of his person, in rebellion against God and exacerbates his state of *original* sin by an *actual* sinfulness personally accepted and fully exercised. The state of "simple" original sin is abolished in him because it is personally assumed. He is damned, not on account of original sin alone, but because of its personal putting into act.

If he makes a positive decision, this man turns, with the same concentrated fullness of his person, towards God, and leaves once and for all the sphere of sinful existentiary being-with, the sphere of original sin (and, of course, his all-embracing decision for God is equivalent in an eminent degree to the desire for baptism). In his case, the state of original sin is abolished by a personal aversion and repression. *In both cases man in his death escapes from the state of simple original sin.*[76]

Thus we see that the hypothesis of a final decision allows us to think of death and its twofold role in the scheme of salvation without any trace of internal contradiction, i.e. not only as punishment, expression and manifestation of sin, but also as the sign of God's mercy and lovingkindness.[77] In this way it enables us to work out for ourselves a unified idea in this truly difficult and complicated problem.

5. The State of Purification

Our efforts to reach greater understanding through these confrontations would be incomplete without a section on the *doctrine of the state of purification*. The fact and the essential nature of purgatory are two among those truths of revelation that have been gradually elaborated in the consciousness of the Church in a constant exchange with the most varied elements contained elsewhere in revelation. The doctrine of purgatory was for a long time contained implicitly, as it were, in other doctrines. It was relatively late before it received its final, clear contours. In view of this, it is not surprising that in some very important points the views of theologians still differ widely. In questions like these, for example: Is purgatory a place? What is its duration? What are the nature and seriousness of the punishment for sin? there is still no real consensus among theologians. The only thing about purgatory that is absolutely certain theologically is the doctrine that every sin a man commits entails a debt of punishment (*reatus poenae*) which cannot simply be paid each time by turning away from the crime committed and nothing else. From this it follows that the essential thing in the process of purification consists in paying this debt of punishment through the pains of satisfaction (*satispassio*). On the other hand there exists no dogmatic declaration of the Church of an obligatory nature dealing with the question whether the imputability of unforgiven venial guilt (*reatus culpae*) can be blotted out in purgatory. This is the point where the expert discussions of theologians usually begin, and this is the point where we should like to take up the problem, which is, of course, connected with the distinction introduced by Peter Lombard (*c.* 1100–60) between the imputability of guilt and the debt of punishment. This treatment will enable us to get to the very heart of the question of purgatory.

The problem is usually stated in the following terms. Let us take the case of a man who dies suddenly in a state of venial sin. How can this man be brought to the beatific vision of God? Not only must the debt of punishment attached to this sin be paid; the guilt itself must be forgiven before the man may enter heaven. This raises a special difficulty. The blotting out of the imputability of guilt is closely bound up with a subjective initiative, that of conversion. Forgiveness of venial sin still present in the subject after death could only be granted in answer to an act of satisfaction on the subject's part calling for and effecting this forgiveness. But in purgatory any possibility of this kind of initiative is denied to human acts, for they have no value as satisfaction, and—at least as far as the subject himself is concerned—fall outside the category of "merit". Accordingly, remission of sin can only take place while man is still in his temporary, provisional state, during his earthly pilgrimage (*in statu viae*), i.e. before death, not after death in the final state (*in statu termini*).

That is, we trust, a fair statement of this classical problem—however strange it may seem. Within the framework of the theological principles indicated, the theologians now try to suggest hypotheses capable of giving a satisfactory answer to the question how venial sins still unforgiven at death can be blotted out before the soul reaches the vision of God.

The first hypothesis we must mention is due to

the great Franciscan theologian Alexander of Hales (*c.* 1170–1245): it assumes that an unconditional forgiveness of all venial sins is granted in this life, apparently immediately before the moment of death. In a gesture of unmerited grace God forgives before death all the venial sins of any man who dies in a state of sanctifying grace.[78] This solution rightly seems inacceptable to most theologians. In the present order of salvation God's gracious lovingkindness always reaches us—as previously pointed out—through the channels of what we subjectively decide. Man must take a real initiative, all his own, though, of course, given in grace. This shows that an unconditional forgiveness is contradictory, perhaps not in itself *ex potentia absoluta*, but certainly in the present order of salvation *ex potentia ordinata*.

So the other great Franciscan theologian, St Bonaventure (1221–74), opposed this conception and suggested another hypothesis contrary to Alexander's.[79] He is of the opinion, though he admits that speculative reasons of great weight are against him, that venial sins are, in spite of everything, forgiven in purgatory itself. In a very slow and painful process, grace gradually permeates the whole reality of the righteous soul in purgatory. This transformation of his existence through grace is supported by the sufferings and the movements of the man himself connected with that suffering. This hypothesis, enunciated in its essential lines by Peter Lombard and taken up again by St Thomas Aquinas in his *Commentary on the Sentences* would seem to recognize in the sufferings of purgatory that character of initiative which, properly speaking, only our time of earthly pilgrimage possesses. For this reason it fails to respect the framework of the theological principles set out earlier.

St Thomas himself, later, in his *Quaestiones Disputatae*,

abandons this view he had accepted in his *Commentary on the Sentences* and attempts to find a half-way solution. His new idea can be summarized as follows. Immediately on the separation of the soul from the body, in the first moment after death, the righteous soul makes an act of perfect charity; this effects the forgiveness of all venial sins; consequently in purgatory only the temporal debt of punishment has to be paid; in this act of charity the soul concentrates the whole of its strength. Now that it is freed from the body the only kind of self-donation of which it is capable is a complete one (not, as formerly, a partial one); strictly speaking this act has not the quality of an initiative and exerts no direct influence on the forgiveness of the venial guilt; but it does indirectly procure the forgiveness of the sin by removing every obstacle in the way of forgiveness.[80]

In spite of the very elegant distinction between the sufferings of satisfaction that are incapable of effecting the forgiveness of venial guilt—"*peccatum veniale quantum ad culpam non remittitur per poenam, quia non est meritoria*"—and the act of charity immediately after death, that only exerts an indirect influence on the forgiveness of the venial guilt by removing the obstacle to forgiveness—"*tollit impedimentum venialis culpae*"—this hypothesis leaves one with the impression that it is doing something very like prolonging the state of pilgrimage beyond death, even if it is only for the space of one single act.

For this reason Cajetan (1469–1534), the commentator on St Thomas, sought to reconstruct his master's intuitions turning them into an essentially new hypothesis. He simply transferred to the moment of death the process described in the *Quaestiones Disputatae*. For Cajetan the moment of death is the final moment of life. Essentially it belongs to the state of pilgrimage in which man is still in a position to take the initiative that is capable of effecting the forgiveness of venial guilt.[81] By this simple transposition to the moment of death of the process of purification by perfect charity, Cajetan was in reality giving us a sketch, not yet elaborated into a system, of the hypothesis of a final decision. If one stops for a moment to consider by what involved trains of thought and with the help of what complicated conceptual constructions the other hypotheses tried to find a reasonably acceptable solution, Cajetan's proposed explanation is refreshing in its sheer simplicity.

This is true; for the hypothesis of a final decision gives us the possibility of thinking of death as a complete opening up to God of our existence. The whole concentrated strength of the righteous soul, now awake to its spirituality, can, in the act of death, be transformed into a flaring up of charity. In this perspective of a final decision man is able to tear himself completely away from himself and meet God in loving devotion. This greatest act of self-devotion would in effect offset all a man's sins and open his heart to God's forgiveness. The only thing remaining would be the debt of temporal punishment in the paying of which defined doctrine sees the essential nature of purgatory.

In this fashion the hypothesis of a final decision provides us with the means for giving a satisfactory and simple solution to one of the most complicated problems of theology. Involuntarily the question arises whether it cannot perhaps give us a good deal more than just that. In the course of history the mysteries of the Christian religion have been, and are still, subject to the universal process of "reification" (*Verdinglichung*, *chosification*) in the theological consciousness. This process can be described as follows.

The original personal fact experienced in a vital encounter comes under the influence of the consciousness and its pictorial projections. It is objectified in images, symbols and representative, descriptive patterns. Processes become "things"; states become "places". The original intentionality in this way acquires a veritable body. These reifying projections are necessary in order that the mind of man may have some sort of consciousness of what it is really aiming at. But at the same time one ought by means of a critically reflective analysis so to reduce the reifying objectifications that the intentionality which finds its expression and comes to consciousness in them is always kept in sight.

The "last things" are particularly subject to this process of reifying objectification. In its decree on purgatory, which is, unfortunately, much too generally neglected, the Council of Trent sharply condemns the excesses of this reifying tendency.[82] Possibly the image of the purifying fire and presentation of the purification itself as a place rather than as a process consisting in a meeting with God may be considered as falling within the definition of a reification that is indispensable if we are to come to a spiritual understanding of the reality. But when the objectification goes further and turns purgatory into a gigantic torture chamber, a cosmic concentration camp in which hapless creatures are punished to an accompaniment of shrieks and groans, then we must affirm that it has overstepped the mark of what can be conceded as legitimate and fallen into grotesque ingenuousness, at the very least. These unworthy imaginings only serve to make the penetration of the mystery the more difficult.

In his remarkable study on purgatory Fr Yves Congar has once again pointed out with great firmness the dangers inseparable from these proceedings.[83] One of the tasks of theological reflexion is to disentangle the primitive spiritual signification of the mysteries from their accumulated reifications. In this sense theological research is always an interiorization and a "de-reification".

The direction in which this reduction should operate in the case of purgatory was indicated as follows by St Augustine, in a very happy dictum in which his particular genius frequently found expression: "After this life God himself is our place."[84] This indicates a twofold reduction in the idea of purgatory: (1) the place to be reduced to a process; (2) the process to be reduced to a personal encounter. The last things and places must be shown to be last processes and the last processes, in their turn, last encounters. "God is the creature's 'last thing'. He is our heaven when we gain him, our hell when we lose him, our judgement when we are examined by him, our purgatory when we are purified by him. He it is at whose contact the finite creature dies, and through whom it rises again to him and in him. But he is all this in the way in which he is turned towards the world, that is, in his Son Jesus Christ, who is the openness of God and, as such, the very concept of the 'last things'."[85] God himself, our meeting with him, is our purgatorial fire. The question now is whether, by any chance, the hypothesis of a final decision gives us the possibility of de-reifying the idea of purgatory and lifting up the whole process of purification into the dimension of an encounter. Is it possible to explain the meeting with the purifying fire of God as a function of the final decision?

We have already indicated that the final decision stands under the sign of a radical stripping down of existence. In making his decision completely for God alone, a man is torn from himself and handed over to God. This breaking up of his existence is in the deepest sense a painful process.

Let us use an example to show this more plainly. In human existence, at the bottom of all we do, there smoulders, like the fire of a volcano, an unceasing attraction of the creature towards God, but this fire is damped down by the layers and rock-formations of our self-seeking, greater in one man, less in another, according to the degree of our inner turning towards our self. Under all these obstacles the fire of God's invitation to his love is buried ever deeper and deeper and only shines through in rare places thanks to the cracks in our existence. But when in our act of final decision our whole capacity for love flames up, then in this outburst of love all the deposits and formations cannot but be broken through. These layers, however, are not something exterior to us; they are the modes of our existence built up in the course of its historical development. That explains why, when the love of God bursts forth, our whole existence has to be broken up—an extremely painful proceeding.

This example is merely meant as an illustration of the fact that the process of integrating man's reality into God's love must of necessity be accompanied by suffering. Our basic decision for God must pierce through all the layers of our reality and carry along with it all that impedes it and slows it down. On the one hand, therefore, the final decision as it turns towards God is the highest act of our love for God and as such capable of effecting the forgiveness of our imputed guilt (*reatus culpae*). On the other hand, it is bound up with suffering and can be included under the concept of the pains of satisfaction (*satispassio*), and even represents a possible means for paying the debt of temporal punishment (*reatus poenae*).

The encounter with God is always painful and entails an upset of our whole existence. There is, indeed, no greater suffering than that caused us by the love of God. We are constantly attracted by God and feel how our existence borne up as by a running tide of being is for ever longing for the presence of God. At the same time, however, in the same act of longing, our soul starts back in terror at the uncanny menace it feels in God. Even here while we are yet pilgrims on earth, we make the painful experience of this twofold character of our love for God. God wounds us.

God's various manifestations of himself in Scripture clearly show this paradoxically composite nature of the encounter with God. Moses veiled his countenance when he beheld the burning bush. He was afraid to look on God.[86] Elijah performed the same symbolic gesture of veiling his face on Mount Horeb.[87] In the vision in which God called Isaiah, even the seraphim veil their faces and the prophet exclaims with the terror of any creature menaced by the Divine: "Woe is me! For I am lost; . . . for my eyes have seen the King, the Lord of hosts!"[88] Daniel saw God in a vision of fire, and the proximity of God caused his whole existence to enter into something like a mystical agony: "When he came, I was frightened and fell upon my face."[89] Ezekiel fell down before God stricken with a strange paralysis and with dumbness.[90] These phenomena are closely related to the great vision of the apostles we call the Transfiguration of Christ:

> Jesus took with him Peter and James and John his brother, and led them up a high mountain apart. And he was transfigured before them, and his face shone like the sun, and his garments became white as light. And behold, there appeared to them Moses and Elijah, talking with him. . . . A bright cloud over-

> shadowed them, and a voice from the cloud said, "This is my beloved Son, with whom I am well pleased; listen to him." When the disciples heard this, they fell on their faces, and were filled with awe.[91]

The intensively experienced proximity of God is full of suffering and danger. It brings with it torment of soul, and a feeling of abandonment and night. To see God face to face is to look into God's eyes of fire. This shakes a man's whole existence, leading it through indescribable suffering. The encounter with God does, of course, cause our souls to burn within us with the maximum of heat, our minds to attain the fullest possible measure of experience, our existences the peak of authenticity. But, at the same time, it burns right into the inner substance of our existence.

One of the fundamental categories of the Johannine experience of Christ is this twofold character of the love of Christ: love and judgement, proximity and remoteness, fulfilment and stripping bare of man—a two-edged sword. These various processes in John's experience of Christ were summed up in the Apocalypse and reduced, we might say, to their essential structure:

> I turned to see the voice that was speaking to me, and on turning I saw . . . one like a son of man . . .; his head and his hair were white as white wool, white as snow; his eyes were like a flame of fire, his feet were like burnished bronze, refined as in a furnace, and his voice was like the sound of many waters; . . . his face was like the sun shining in full strength. When I saw him, I fell at his feet as though dead.[92]

All these events can serve as pictorial indications of what may, presumably, occur in the final decision and the encounter with God this makes possible. Christ looks with utter love and complete graciousness upon the man who comes to him. At the same time his gaze burns right into the innermost parts of that human existence. To encounter God in Christ's eyes of fire is the highest fulfilment of our capacity for love and also the most fearful suffering our nature ever has to bear. Seen in this way, purgatory would be the passage, which we effect in our final decision, through the purifying fire of divine love. The encounter with Christ would be our purgatory.[93]

There still remains a last question to clear up in this interpretation of the process of purification. There is a certain contradiction in the fact that we place in the final decision both the forgiveness of the guilt and the remission of the punishment. In the case of the first, it is supposed that the final decision belongs to the state of our pilgrimage (*status viae*); in the latter case, with the removal of purgatory and its situating in the dimension of the final decision, the contradictory statement is made: since purgatory must be considered as belonging to the final state (*status termini*), the final decision must also be transferred to the same final state. But is it possible for the final decision to extend at one and the same time over both the state of pilgrimage and the final state? Yes, it is; but from essentially different points of view.

Right at the beginning of our methodological investigations[94] we tried to show that death, as an instantaneous change, entails the reciprocal interpenetration of two moments: the last moment before death and the first moment after death. The very absence of any temporality from the transition effected in death means that the moments of separating (*separari*) and of being separated (*separatum esse*) coincide, forming a single composite and temporal entity. The metaphysical structure of instantaneous change was more than once described by St Thomas Aquinas,[95] and applied to several problems in speculative theology, e.g. the processes of creation and illumination, eucharistic consecration and justification of the sinner.[96] The same metaphysical consideration occurs to him when he is dealing with other theological questions of a related kind.[97]

If we attempt to discover the essential structure of St Thomas's enquiries, we discover two things: (1) in instantaneous changes the moments of before and after interpenetrate each other; (2) in an instantaneous process a rich and intense spiritual activity can be exercised. If we now apply these considerations analogically to the hypothesis of a final decision it will no longer appear unthinkable that the process of death—which is composed by the moments of separating and being separated—and the final decision made during it should, according as one considers the one or the other of the two aspects, belong to the state of pilgrimage (offering thus a possibility for the forgiveness of guilt), and, on the other hand, already penetrate into the final state (providing therefore the place where the debt of punishment can be paid).

To sum up, we could say of our theological confrontation that the hypothesis of a final decision offers a satisfactory answer to the question of the forgiveness of the imputability of venial guilt still present at the time of death. Through its metaphysical extension into the state of pilgrimage the final decision still belongs to the sphere in which this forgiveness can be obtained. Furthermore, the hypothesis of a final decision enables us to conceive of the state of purification as a dimension of the last, final meeting with Christ. Through its second metaphysical extension into the final state, the final decision enables us to explain purgatory as an integration, by means of an encounter, of the many layers of our human reality into the overpowering love of God, a love so devouring that it causes acute suffering to the unpurified man. We see now that the hypothesis of a final decision opens up horizons within the limits of which a deep theological interiorization of the doctrine of purgatory can be achieved.

6. *Christological Basis for the Hypothesis of a Final Decision*

To conclude, we should like to set out the *christological basis* for the conception of death here proposed. It is a constant conviction of the Christian Church founded on the statements of Scripture, the tradition of the Fathers and the general teaching of the Church, that Christ saved us by his death, not in any other way. Primarily, it is true, we were justified through Christ's obedience, but through an obedience "even unto death". It was in death that there occurred that transference of Christ's whole creaturely being which is the sublime expression of his obedience. Through the free gift of his life, Christ offered the sacrifice by means of which fallen man was reconciled with God. Death is the "It is accomplished" of Christ's work of salvation, because it was the complete manifestation of his obedience. What is the reason for this insistent emphasis on the importance of Christ's death in the work of redemption? Why could not any moral act on the part of Christ, an act that would have infinite value in virtue of the infinite dignity of the divine person, become a complete and adequate expression of Christ's redeeming obedience? Why did this obedience have to be paid to death?

Merely to invoke God's free disposition of all things as an answer to this question seems a very feeble speculative attitude. No indication of this sort can be considered as pressing forward to the ultimate reasons for Christ's death. On the one hand, there is no need whatever to take refuge in a disposition of God, until we have exhausted all the possibilities contained in the reason for the thing itself. On the other hand, God's disposition cannot simply be regarded without further examination as the sole basis. God's free disposition always has an immanent objectification precisely in its object. Hence it (the disposition) can be demonstrated through the appropriate reduction of the ontological structure of the object itself as a thing. It follows that we can accept an invocation of God's free disposition as a sufficient basis only if we proceed further in our investigation and take pains to deduce the why of this disposition—in so far as we can—from the structure of the object, in this case, the death of Christ. The hypothesis of a final decision seems quite extraordinarily adapted for bringing to light an intrinsic reason in this troublesome question. Our proof contains four points.

Firstly: Our starting-point is the Thomist teaching on the physical instrumental causality of Christ's human nature in the work of redemption. His human reality is the instrument of the Godhead (*instrumentum divinitatis*) in the actions of Christ. "Human nature is assumed in Christ in order that it may accomplish as an instrument things that are acts proper to God alone, as cleansing from sin, enlightening minds through grace, introduction into the perfection of eternal life. So then, Christ's human nature is compared to God as a proper and conjoined (*proprium et coniunctum*) instrument, like the hand compared to the soul."[98] In another connexion St

Thomas Aquinas emphasizes strongly that the *instrumentum divinitatis* does not lose the least part of its specific activity through its close association with the guiding and moving influence of the divinity.[99] So then, the more perfect the human nature of Christ, the more apt it is for the effecting of the redemption of which it is the instrumental cause.

Now, it is certain beyond all doubt that although the human reality of Christ, from the first moment of its existence, was already at the goal of man's earthly pilgrimage, yet—seen from another point of view—it was still in its state of pilgrimage (the classical formula of christology says: "*Christus simul viator et comprehensor*"), and could consequently advance from the imperfect to the perfect. Theology has made this abundantly clear with reference to Christ's acquired human knowledge. Christ possessed a real human nature. But to this reality belongs of necessity a capacity for knowledge open to real progress. For Christ the *viator* it was of capital importance that he should not lack that very mode of knowledge that characterizes man in his state of pilgrimage. If we are really going to exclude all trace of docetism, then progress for Christ in acquired human knowledge cannot be understood in the sense of a mere progressive revelation *ad extra* of Christ's wisdom. It must be a real increase of his acquired knowledge.

In the person of Christ, alongside the divine will, there is also a true human will (dyotheletism). That being so, we can apply by analogy the line of argumentation we have just been explaining, to Christ's human volition, for in its exercise this follows very closely on knowledge; not, of course, supposing it to be a progressive freeing from the passions, but a field of experience gained through experience and spreading ever more widely in dependence on the increase of acquired knowledge. Connected with the acts of assimilation of the world (knowledge) and of the efficient appetite for the good (volition), there is in the spiritual life of man another wider circle of functions: the realm of the emotions. Knowledge and volition in man are clothed in and permeated by feelings. We must, therefore, assume that with regard to Christ's human emotional life an authentic progress occurs in his advancement towards spiritual adulthood.

Now if, as the hypothesis of a final decision emphasizes, the being that is man reaches the climax of his adulthood only in death, we can understand why it is in death that Christ's humanity became the perfect instrumental cause of our redemption, and why it is in death that it effected that full self-surrender to the Father, that reconciled us with God. Of course, the perfecting of Christ's human knowledge, volition and emotional life in death does not signify any increase in merit—every action of Christ's humanity, finite by its being, has infinite value in virtue of the hypostatic union—but it does certainly mean an increase in the perfecting of its instrumentality. Christ is man and as *viator* was not able to give full human expression to his redemptive obedience until he did so in death. His death effects our salvation because in it is summed up all the fullness of the human expression of Christ's obedience. The developing human reality of Christ, according to the hypothesis of a final decision, attains its perfection, and consequently the perfection of its instrumentality also, only in death. Thus the perspective of the hypothesis of a final decision provides us with the possibility of finding an intrinsic reason for the fact that Christ's redemptive obedience should be given to death and in death.[100]

Secondly: The next step in our demonstration is a

prolongation, wholly in accordance with its original meaning, of St Thomas's teaching on the instrumental causality of Christ's humanity we have just dealt with. Within Christ's human reality we can discover different levels of being interconnected one with another by an instrumental causality of their own. Our Lord's corporal reality constitutes the last link in the chain of instrumental causes by means of which the Logos accomplishes the work of redemption. The Council of Ephesus (431) speaks in its eleventh Anathematism of the Lord's "lifegiving flesh" (ζωοποιὸς σάρξ).[101] This expresses the long tradition of the Greek Fathers which saw in Christ's body the organ or instrument of the Logos in the work of redemption.[102]

Theologians of the Thomist school of thought also call upon the Greek tradition for confirmation, when they develop their theory of the instrumental causality of Christ's body, e.g. on Eusebius and St John Damascene. In his *Commentary on the Sentences*, St Thomas clearly expresses his conception: "The flesh is said to be 'divinized', not as though it had become the Godhead itself, but because it has become God's flesh and because, thanks to its union with the Godhead, it possesses more abundantly the gifts of the Godhead, and because to a certain extent it is a tool by means of which the divine power works our salvation. So he conferred healing, when he touched the leper with his flesh, through the power of his Godhead, and dying in the flesh, he conquered death through his divine power. But the power of the person who acts is, after a certain fashion, in the tool by means of which he performs his act."[103]

This profound theory, so important for our grasp of what salvation really is, was seized upon by devout Christians with a kind of instinctive approval and has been put into practice for ages. The Christian in his prayers turns spontaneously to Christ's bodily reality. Without being able to invoke reasons of speculative theology, he nevertheless senses that the humanity of Christ has, as it were, absorbed, and thus neutralized, the dangers of man's meeting with God. In Christ's countenance the believer can behold the divinity without its fatal menace of death. The unveiled vision of the Godhead pervades the whole human existence of Christ and is no longer terrifying. On the contrary, it is seen as a thing of indescribable charm and kindliness.

The gently hesitant gesture of the unfortunate woman of Capernaum who touched the hem of Christ's garment ever so lightly,[104] has always been the essential attitude of Christian mysticism. Even where devotional life following the general movement of mystical interiorization does not seize upon the personality of Christ in all the manifold richness of its concrete appearance among us, but rather narrows it down into summarized, comprehensive concepts—an example of this mystical unification of the multiple can be found in Gregory the Great's *Dialogues*, 2, 23, where we read that St Benedict once saw the whole varied splendour of the cosmos gathered together in one ray of light—even in such cases, the really Christian concentration of devotion on the corporeity of Christ is not only preserved; it can even be said to reach its climax. For example, the "mind" of Christ, the most intimate aspect of his most deeply personal attitude, is seized on in the symbol of the heart and developed in the richly varied devotion to the Sacred Heart.[105]

If Christ's bodily reality is the physical instrumental cause of grace, and if every grace is christological, then in the production of every grace, we must include its physical communication through Christ's body. Even St Thomas fought shy of the radicality of this conclusion. Presumably he did not feel capable of explaining how our Lord's bodily reality can enter into physical contact with the men of all ages and all places. Yet this general possibility of contact with Christ is an absolutely essential condition, because every man, by the simple fact of being a man, is under the grace of Christ.

St Thomas endeavoured to evade the difficulty by elaborating the following distinction. Christ's bodily reality possesses a spiritual power which comes from its union with the divinity, but this power works, not through physical contact, but through "spiritual contact", viz. in faith and in the sacraments of faith.[106] We have, of course, to maintain that the contact with Christ must be, of absolute necessity, a "spiritual" one; but this does not do away with the requirement of the "bodily contact". The two are not mutually exclusive. The spiritual contact should rather be seen as a mode of the bodily contact.

The miracle of healing in Capernaum shows us plainly that the spiritual contact is the intensity of faith with which the physical contact is made. Christ is surrounded by a crowd, jostled and greedily clutched at from all sides. One sick woman lightly touched the hem of his garment. Power went out from the Lord and made him ask: "Who touched my garment?" "Why do you ask such things?" they answered. "Can you not see how the crowd presses on you?" They did not understand the mystery. Though many may have been handling him in a merely bodily way, only one touched him really. She touched him with a drawing-near of everything that made up her existence, a drawing-near that was both physical and spiritual. This demonstrates that spiritual encounter is a dimension of faith contained in the bodily contact.

This gives us the problem in the following form. Through the work of redemption accomplished in his death Christ effected an existentiary transformation of mankind in its totality and set it on its way towards its supernatural end. If that is so, he came, by the very fact of his death, into physical and bodily contact with all men, for Christ's activity in the distribution and communication of grace is always realized in a bodily contact. Our task, therefore, is to find in Christ's death-process a significant fact capable of explaining to us how Christ is in contact with all men. The solution of this problem on all its many levels—we must, alas, give up any idea of developing it here in all its dimensions—is greatly facilitated by the hypothesis of a final decision.

In the philosophical part of this study one of the things we set out was the aspect of the hypothesis of a final decision according to which man in his death enters upon a real ontological relationship with the universe.[107] In death the soul is firmly planted in that basis of unity which is at the root of the world. The soul's freeing from the body in death does not just mean a withdrawal from matter. Rather does it signify the entering into a closer proximity with matter, into a relation with the world extended to cosmic proportions. In this connexion the imaginative concept "the heart of the earth" or "the heart of the universe" was formed to describe the metaphysical place where this total presence to the world occurs. In this way the act of death as seen in the hypothesis of a final decision will be a descent into the unity at the root of the world. It is to be noted that Christ himself called his descent in death an entry into "the heart of the earth" (ἐν τῇ καρδίᾳ τῆς γῆς).[108] If we now try to apply this insight about the entry of the soul into a pancosmic relationship with the world to Christ's *descent into hell*, we shall understand better why and how the bodily, human reality of Christ became in death rather than in any other way the instrumental cause of all grace.

This would immediately suggest the conception according to which Christ's sojourn in hell is explained as something arising out of the nature of his death. Christ's descent "into the lower parts of the earth"[109] would not be thought of only as a work of redemption on Christ's part for those men of the ages before Christ who were saved;[110] it would also be explained as the creating of a new situation in the scheme of salvation for the whole of humanity, and, indeed, as a re-fashioning of the world's evolution beginning at its deepest basis. As in the hypothesis of a final decision, Christ's human soul in death would have entered into an open, concrete ontological relationship with the universe. This means that the cosmos in its totality would have become the bodily instrument of Christ's humanity and the instrumental cause of the divine efficacy, for every creature that belongs corporeally to this cosmos.

When, in the way we have just explained, Christ's human reality was planted, in death, right at the heart of the world, within the deepest stratum of the universe, the stratum that unites at root bottom all that the world is, at that moment in his bodily humanity he became the real ontological ground of a new universal scheme of salvation embracing the whole human race.[111]

Henceforth, all men without exception can enter into bodily contact with Christ, and precisely by means of the cosmic reality with which each man is so intimately connected. (Existence, of course, *exists* in a state of transcendental reference to the world.) The world is the essential dimension of every spiritual activity of man, whose soul is bound up with material being in a single substantial unity. But if Christ in his manhood has been planted in the basis of the world, the substantial unity of the human soul with material being has been changed ontologically. The whole of our personal assimilation of the world has received through this fact a new, divine dimension. Perhaps this might help us to explain better why our world is so deeply and mysteriously filled with the reality of Christ, and why man in his spiritual and personal life, when all is said and done and whether he knows it or not, is always concerned with Christ.

If then, we consider the descent into hell from the point of view of the hypothesis of a final decision, we see that at Christ's death the whole world entered upon a cosmic spring the harvest of which will be the remaking of our universe in newness and splendour at the end of time. At the moment of Christ's death the veil of the temple was rent in two from top to bottom, the veil, that is, that hung before the Holy of Holies.[112] For Jewish mysticism and subsequently in the Christian interpretation of this mysterious happening, the veil of the temple represented the whole universe as it stands between God and man.[113] This veil was torn in two at Christ's death to show us that, at the moment when Christ's act of redemption is consummated, the whole cosmos opens itself to the Godhead, bursts open for God like a flower-bud. In his triumphant descent into the innermost fastnesses of the world the Son of God tore open the whole world and made it transparent to God's light; nay, he made of it a vehicle of sanctification. In that moment the movement that had been going on for thousands of millions of years, the sighing and groaning of creation reached their end. The universe is no longer what it was before. This transformation of the world is even now an already existent reality.

During this present "betwixt and between", however, i.e. the time of salvation stretching from the descent of Christ to the Parousia, the universe is still looking expectantly for the final revelation of what has already been done in the depths of the world's being. Even now we are living our lives in a world penetrated from its innermost centre and basis with glory; we sense that the whole cosmos bathes in the light of the Godhead. Even now, out of our world, divine life flows towards us. We are also being borne along unceasingly towards God on the breast of a boundless flood-tide of the universe. Christ is already at work in us from the centre of the world, and we ourselves, albeit usually unconsciously, are doing God's work in our character as creatures of the world. All this belongs to the dimension of Christ's descent into the deepest depths of all things visible, which he achieved in death. So, Christ's bodily humanity became in death the instrumental cause of a fundamentally new situation in the scheme of salvation for all those spirits which through their corporeity belong to the world and have an essential reference to being in the world.[114]

This interpretation of Christ's sojourn in the underworld differs in no way from the usual conception of the descent into hell as professed in the fifth article of the Apostles' Creed. Quite on the contrary, it seems to us to be rather a thematic unfolding and unravelling of what is implicitly contained in the classical conception of the descent into hell. Let us now demonstrate this fundamental identity of both conceptions with the help of two illustrations.

Firstly: It is worth considering that in the imaginative pattern of the journey into hell—descent into the *depths*, the *underworld*, the *innermost* parts of the earth—there is contained, implicitly at least, another pattern: "Man, when he goes down into hell, enters, in some sort, into the deepest stratum of the world's reality, the stratum that unites all things at root bottom."[115] According to this, then, Christ's descent has always been thought of and existentially put into practice, if not explicitly at least by implication, as an entering into the realm of the inward, the interior, the essential.

The movements of being, seen in the imagination as spatial movements, occur in a "space of existence", this term designating not merely the whole complex of bodily relationships, but also the structure of the metaphysical world-edifice. Descent is a figure taken from the imaginative pattern of a geocentric system in which the whole cosmos is represented as a sphere having in its centre the earth, likewise a spherical body. In the "upper world" far above all spheres is God's non-spatial abode, the Empyrean. The centre of the terrestrial globe is the bottommost "lowest" of all things, opposed to the Empyrean. The depths of the world are the place where everything that is of this world's substance—not only the cosmic relationship, but also the psychic connexions—finds its centre and interiority. This makes of it the interiority of the whole cosmos and the interiority of the human heart.

If, then, we consider the incarnation of Christ in this metaphysical space-pattern, the descent of the Logos from the Empyrean on to the surface of the earth appears as the beginning of his world conquest. In order that Christ may be able to establish his sway over the whole world, he has a still more essential descent to make—right down to the central point of all worldly connexions, the centre of the earth, i.e. the innermost heart and core of the whole cosmos. Seen thus Christ's entry into hell is the required prolongation of the descent he made in his incarnation.

But this also means that if the hypothesis of a final decision gives us the interpretation of Christ's descent into hell as an entry into a pancosmic world relationship, this interpretation, nevertheless, lies perfectly in the line of thought of the classical representation of the descent into hell.

A second illustration: In his death Christ disarmed and reduced to powerlessness[116] those principalities and powers[117] that had their place in the innermost seclusion, the essential structure of the world, as the principles, permanent forces and elements of the cosmos. Their essential nature was hidden from man's limited vision, but they ruled over the world processes, and allowed their presence to be discerned in all the phenomena of the world and of existence, of both of which they had obtained possession.

Exegetes differ as to whether these principalities and powers overcome in Christ's death were good or evil. O. Cullmann and H. Schlier think they were evil, P. Benoit, good; L. Cerfaux considers that they were indeterminate. "On the one hand it was a providential order of things that was abolished in the dispossession of the angelic governors: but as this constitution had been corrupted through the work of the fallen angels, the catastrophe also wears the appearance of a victory on Christ's part over the insurgent powers of darkness."[118] One thing, however, is certain: in his death Christ inaugurated a new state of the world and established a pancosmic kingly dominion which is already a reality embracing all the dimensions of the cosmos and of existence.

The intermediary powers in God's rule over cosmos and existence are now done away with once and for all, though certain angelic powers in spite of their dethronement do seem to retain some degree of authority until

Christ's second coming and must, therefore, be overcome by the faithful themselves.[119] In Christ's death they were definitively deprived of that place as his lieutenants which God had given them in his original dispensation. Christ's death, therefore, introduced a reshaping of the whole universe which began at its innermost basis. Behind the phenomena of nature and the events of history there no longer stand the principalities and powers. Christ himself is now mysteriously present to and with us through his cosmos. Thus he became the innermost centre of all the *fieri* of history. He took over the place of the angelic powers at the innermost roots of the whole visible creation. The whole universe was filled with his being as God-Man. From the metaphysical depths of the universe new, divinized forces are already flowing into our existential environment on the outer surface of things. Christ is in the depths of the whole creation because he has occupied the position of the principles and elements of the world. This position in the universe which he has conquered for himself by disarming the elements of this world in his death, will only be made finally manifest to us at the Second Coming.

Seen from this second, Pauline point of view, our interpretation of Christ's sojourn in hell as his entering into the basis of the world and the creation of a fundamentally new cosmic situation in the scheme of salvation—of an "existentiary" situation, valid for all men, laying hold physically of all earth-bound spirits, and operating through the fact of our essential state of reference to the world—seems to be remarkably close to the original conception of the descent into hell.

One of the most important results we owe to Pierre Teilhard de Chardin's efforts in the world of thought is the opening up for Christian spirituality of the christological dimensions of our essential belonging to the world. The basic intuition both of his proposed world-system and of the spiritual teaching which can be built up on the basis of his *Milieu divin* and the indications scattered here and there in his various books and letters,[120] consists in the assertion that we can meet Christ everywhere because throughout the whole universe an essential Christ dimension, an *élément christique* is to be found. The experience of the immersion of the whole cosmic *fieri* in Christ's human reality is the key to the thought of Teilhard de Chardin. In his world-picture Christ is everywhere present in evolution with his whole creative efficacy as the most intimate of all the energies at work in the process. The universe is a vessel and an abode of the divine. In the most literal sense of the term it is a *milieu divin*. The whole evolving cosmos is a transparency of Christ, which is why we can discover Christ at the heart of all things and happenings with his reality as God-Man. For the Christian, therefore, communion with the world is a communion with this inner reality of all visible things, Jesus Christ. Thus the Christian is able to perceive the traces of the divine presence in the world again, not however, this time, in a symbolical ascent of the soul through creation to God. This is how mediaeval spirituality raised men's minds to God, but we have largely lost the mediaeval view of the world, so that for us it must be a question of throwing oneself into a world which is constantly growing into God's dimensions, and which is, indeed, in a hidden and mysterious way, already the dimension of the divine. Perhaps the interpretation of Christ's descent into the "heart of the universe" which this essay is proposing may serve to provide a theological foundation for the exciting and inspiring discovery made in Teilhard's spirituality of the "cosmic Christ" in whom we and, with us, all things are and exist.

Thirdly: Still from the point of view of the hypothesis of a final decision, it seems to me absolutely indispensable that we should situate, at least tentatively, in and with the events of Christ's death I have described, the two further processes essentially connected therewith, viz. the resurrection and the ascension. In his descent into the innermost parts of the world Christ created a new situation in the scheme of salvation for all those spirits who by their corporeity are established in a reference to the universe, since these spirits, precisely in virtue of their link with the world, are, from the moment of Christ's death, in bodily contact with his human reality. In the dogma of the resurrection and ascension it seems to the present writer that we may see an explicit laying-bare of two strands present in the reality already accomplished in principle by Christ in his descent into hell. Here, in brief, are the reasons for this view.

Firstly, as regards the *resurrection* and what happened in it. Before his death Christ existed in what Johannine theology calls "the flesh", the domain of weakness and frailty, the existential relationship of a cramped, sealed-off visible thing bound as it were to a definite spatio-temporal place. In the process of his death Christ finally laid aside the "fleshly" components of his visibility and entered into the universe in its wholeness with its openness of being. This meant that the whole world was introduced into a clarified system of being, into the dimension of the "pneumatic". The ultimate finality of a world permeated and transformed by the spirit has dawned. The end of time, the universal transfiguration has come. Our world and what it is has already become essentially heaven. But, this fundamental transfiguration of being is still hidden awaiting its revelation at the end of time. The great sign that this working of the spirit into and through all being has indeed already taken place in spite of all its veiling from us, is given us in Christ's risen body. This is a body permeated by the spirit and removed from the domain of cramped, transitory, impermanent things, sealed off into particular compartments and present through being tied to conditions of time and space. Christ's transfigured body is the archetype of the universe as already introduced in a mysterious and hidden way into the state of transfiguration, and also of the human race as permeated by the spirit and eschatologically unified. It is the ontological expression of Christ's descent and of what happened in this descent. It is also the essence of our bodily contact with Christ. Free of all the "fleshly" constraints of time and place, Christ is able to reach the men of all times and places and make them members of his transfigured body, i.e. enable them to participate in his "pneumatic" corporeity. Any man who by reason of a personally realized donation has entered through Christ's body into union with the Godhead is one of the redeemed and is in communion with God.

The glorification realized in the resurrection, i.e. Christ's entry into the unimpeded, open clarity of being, is, therefore, an event in the scheme of salvation. It procures the condition for the possibility of our salvation because it enables us to grow together with the risen body of Christ, and this growing together with Christ is precisely what salvation is.[121] Descent into the interior of all visible creation, and resurrection as an entry into the pneumatic openness of the corporeal, are, therefore, two reciprocally interpenetrating aspects of the one passage through death of Christ.[122]

In this consideration we have been able to demonstrate, with the aid of the hypothesis of a final decision, first of all, the immanent redemptivity of Christ's death; further, by following the same reasoning, to interpret Christ's descent as a dimension of that passage through death; and finally, to see in the resurrection the real ontological expression in concrete shape of what was accomplished in Christ's descent.

Something similar could be attempted in endeavouring to explain the *ascension* and what happened in it. The Johannine theology of "exaltation" suggests the idea that the act of ascension and the events of death and resurrection are to be regarded as factors in one and the same event seen as a whole. "I, when I am lifted up from the earth, will draw all men to myself"; so says St John's Gospel in the decisive text.[123] The expressions "exaltation", "lifting up" and "raising up" with their Johannine overtones refer both to Christ's death as an "exaltation on the cross" and also to the "raising up into heaven" in the framework of the resurrection.

The most obvious meaning of Christ's going up into heaven would, therefore, be his entry at the resurrection into that divine world that for our human imagination is the world of heaven above the earth. Through the resurrection the glorified Christ enters, of necessity, into the sphere of God's glory. For this reason, all except two of the New Testament texts—and we shall deal with the two exceptions in a moment—treat Christ's being in heaven as the immediate consequence of his resurrection.[124] They are two aspects of one and the same glorious triumphal progress of Christ, two aspects that are inseparable, linked together by an essential, intrinsic necessity and coincident in time. The going up into heaven is a return to the Father, a progress terminating in the sitting in glory at the right hand of the Father, and a leaving behind of life in the flesh. A single process is meant in all this, and of the various elements that make it up: death, descent, resurrection and ascension, each singles out and emphasizes one aspect of a single web of happening.

In Hebrews 9, this composite and single process is hinted at in the image of a man walking the length of the temple all the way to the sanctuary which is the final term of Christ's advance towards his sacrifice: "For Christ has entered, not into a sanctuary made with hands, a copy of the true one, but into heaven itself, now to appear in the presence of God on our behalf."[125] In this fourfold and yet single process of Christ's exaltation there occurred Christ's integral act of transcending and breaking through all the barriers of "fleshly" corporeity, filling the whole universe with his royal presence. "He . . . ascended far above all the heavens, that he might fill all things."[126] Christ's ascension, therefore, is the final accomplishment of that presence in which we have already found the truest meaning of both the descent into hell and the resurrection to reside, the universal presence of Christ in the universe.

St Luke's account of the ascension[127] does, however, raise certain objections against this interpretation. In it we are expressly told that Christ did not enter into heaven immediately on his resurrection, but did so forty days later when he rose up in a visible ascent from the Mount of Olives. There is a very simple distinction that can dissipate these objections.

The New Testament offers us a double series of texts: on the one hand, all the texts that represent the ascension as the immediate continuation of the resurrection; on the other hand, the witness of St Luke that the ascension did not occur until forty days later. We shall best do justice to these two series if we assume that there were two clearly distinguished aspects of the ascension: (1) the exaltation of Christ to the Father in heaven coinciding both in essence and in time with the resurrection; (2) the visible revelation of his departure on the Mount of Olives. "Christ's appearances were appearances of the Risen Lord already in the state of his final glory. And so the leave-taking of Jesus from his disciples on the Mount of Olives was nothing but the sign, perceptible to men's eyes, of the finality of the glory into which Christ had entered through his resurrection."[128]

Seen in this way, Christ's departure forty days after his resurrection is a sign that he is now seated at the right hand of the Father, that the period of intimate association with him is over, and that he will come no more until the Parousia. The very considerable waverings of early Christian tradition as to the time of the ascension can be quoted in support of this interpretation. Not until the fourth century did the account in Acts secure the general adherence of the Fathers,[129] and this development is essentially liturgical in origin. The primitive Church celebrated Easter and Pentecost as a single feast lasting fifty days. Until the fourth century there was no special Feast of the Ascension. Our first homilies for the Ascension were left by Saints Gregory of Nyssa (*c.* 330 – *c.* 395) and John Chrysostom (*c.* 347–407).[130]

The ascension as an inner dimension of the resurrection, having as its outward sign the ascent from the Mount of Olives forty days later—this is a view which quite obviously takes into account all the facts of the theology of the ascension.

Let us now summarize our considerations on the

christological basis of the hypothesis of a final decision. We find a picture of Christ's passage through death of marked inner coherence. In his death Christ attained the perfect accomplishment of his reality as man with a human body and soul, and consequently, the perfect instrumental causality of his humanity. Therefore, and precisely in his death, he was able to effect our salvation finally and irrevocably. This is his *death.*

At the same time, however, his death was a penetration into the open clarity of the universe, and by this means, he created a fundamentally new situation in the scheme of salvation for all spirits which, by reason of their corporeity, are substantially united with material being. This is his *descent into hell.*

The world reshaped in Christ's death at the heart of its innermost essential basis finds its perfected expression in the body of Christ delivered from all the bonds of flesh and clarified in all its being. By its removal from all limitations of time and place Christ's body makes it possible for us to reach our salvation in a growing together with him. This is his *resurrection.*

This means that Christ, even in his body, is henceforth in the realm of being proper to God and has thus become the ultimate fulfilment of the cosmos, the point *omega* of an evolution pressing ever further forward in the power of God into the sphere of the divine. This is the *ascension.*

The death of Christ is, therefore, the passage, i.e. passover, composed of these four essential elements, from the realm of the provisional to the state of divine clarity. In this way the hypothesis of a final decision has enabled us to work our way through to a unifying, general view of the basic process of our redemption.[131]

Now, if we join this last train of thought with the

conclusions of our philosophical analysis and thus try to express the essential result of our whole investigation into the mystery of death, we come to the following summary statement: Man's death is a *sacramental situation*. This last insight ought now to make plain, in a cumulative way, all we have said hitherto, bringing together both parts of the investigation, the philosophical and the theological, in one unifying vision.

On the one hand, at the close of our philosophical reflexions on human death we came to see that in death the soul is confronted with the totality of its subjective dynamism of being (death as total self-encounter), by entering completely into the pancosmic world-relationship, into the basis of the world (death as total presence to the world). These two determinations did not, however, designate two separate processes, but rather two aspects, one formal and the other material, of one and the same happening. In death the soul takes hold of itself completely and realizes in so doing its reference to this world, a reference "given" in its being as a transcendental determinism and even now always posited in its concrete being. By coming fully to itself it reaches its integral relativity to the world. Or, expressed as seen from the other side of the process, but just as rightly and truly: the soul becomes identified with its total relationship with the world and reaches in this the plenitude of its self-encounter. In these two essential "moments" of death is realized a single situation of being: the plenitude of being lights up brightly before the human existence. In death the soul reaches the place where the whole complex of being, that of the individual's own dynamism of existence as well as that of the whole cosmos, joins up with the Godhead.

This essential situation of being is even so not yet the

total of what can be attained. Fulfilment can only come from a decision taken in this situation of being. The situation of death is, therefore, only a "last but one" that bears in itself an essential indication pointing to the real "last" that makes total fulfilment possible, and is, therefore, the sign as being of this fulfilment. In the situation of death there shines forth in broken rays something that is already the pure fullness of light of the spiritual world. Let us point out once again three factors: (1) in death the concrete human existence is transferred into a situation of being that is the sign showing the nature of the final fulfilment; (2) this situation of being contains as its formal element an all-embracing self-encounter of the soul; (3) its material structural factor is a total presence to the world in death.

On the other hand, the reasonings of our theological investigation have led us to understand that this essential situation of being that is death's, is the place of the total encounter with Christ. Christ's fourfold and single act: death, descent, resurrection and ascension, by means of which he accomplished our redemption has reshaped the whole cosmos christologically and made of it an instrument of the Godhead (*instrumentum divinitatis*). In his death Christ with his sacred humanity became present to the whole universe as the innermost and deepest part of all that is the world. Therefore, the material element of the human death-situation has become a vehicle of Christ. But since, by reason of its transcendental relativity to the world, the soul is bound up with the cosmos, this presence of Christ in the cosmos penetrates right into the innermost fibres of man's spiritual dynamism. In his death, therefore, Christ has not only transformed the objective reality of the world as it is; he has also set the subjective dynamism of the human spirit as being, on its way towards its supernatural end, and at the same time reshaped it ontologically, so that Christ himself stands henceforth at the immanent focal point of all the spiritual aspirations of man. Everything we have ever guessed at, sensed and loved, is united in him as in a single centre of meaning. That is why the formal element of the human death-situation is a christologically reshaped reality. When, therefore, the soul is planted, in death, in the basis of the world and also awakens to the totality of its spirituality, it seizes—in both elements of its death-situation, the material (complete presence to the world) and the formal (total self-encounter)—Christ himself as the one who is essentially present in its totally realized relationship with the world and with itself. So the death-situation of the concrete human existence is a sign of its encounter with Christ. In the logical prolongation of the totally experienced relationship with the world and of the consciously known dynamism of the spirit stands Christ, his presence shining brightly through both the material and the formal elements of the process of death. Death, therefore, is *an encounter with Christ realized in the essential sign of the basis of the world and of the spiritual dynamism of man.*

Since the sacraments themselves are encounters with Christ realized in signs of being that are human, i.e. composed of personal (formal) and worldly (material) elements, we can conclude from what has been said that death is an eminently sacramental situation.[132]

The "sacrament" of death. This must not be thought of as a new individual sacrament, of course. On the one hand, the fact that there are seven sacraments has been dogmatically defined; on the other hand, death as an elevation on to an essentially higher plane of all the acts of life cannot be put in the same category as the other acts of life, among which we must, of course, reckon our meetings with Christ in the individual sacraments. Death should be looked on rather as a "basic sacrament", mysteriously present in the other sacraments and inwardly supporting them at the same time as it transcends them. As the supreme, most decisive, clearest and most intimate encounter with Christ of a man's whole life, death summarizes all the other encounters, concentrating in itself the whole spiritual history of a man and facing him once more with a decision. All the sacraments are effective in so far as they communicate a physical contact with the one fundamental sacrament of all salvation, Christ's human reality. This physical contact with Christ's humanity reaches its final intensity in death, since the whole spiritual dynamism of man and the cosmos experienced as a whole become transparent when seen against the light of Christ. This is the deepest and truest meaning of the hypothesis: *Death is man's first completely personal act, and is, therefore, by reason of its very being, the centre above all others for the awakening of consciousness, for freedom, for the encounter with God, for the final decision about one's eternal destiny.*

7. *Summary of the Theological Discussion*

In this third chapter of our work, we have six times called on our philosophically elaborated hypothesis of a final decision to throw light on theological problems. In doing so we have adopted the *method of theological research* recommended by the First Vatican Council: a basic philosophical thought was set to work as an hypothesis to see if it would furnish new light on certain articles of faith and bring into greater mutual agreement a number of dogmatic data often treated in quite dissimilar ways. This was nothing more than a theological essay, in the etymological and modest, but none the less confident, sense of the word.

As our first meeting-point for the philosophical hypothesis and the problem of theology we chose the *finality of the state we reach through death.* With death man's time of trial and probation comes to an end, and his existence enters into a final state in which his basic attitude as regards his salvation can no more be changed. But why does the time for the possible revision of our decisions end with death? The explanations which derive from the ideas either of a special intervention of God or of an immanent appetite for being on the part of human volition, do not really take into account all the complexity of the problem. The hypothesis of a final decision enables us to understand the fixation in its ultimate finality of the state reached after death—whether damnation or eternal bliss—as a factor of our liberty itself. The final decision, whatever it may be, realizes all at once the whole plenitude of a man's dynamism of existence and exhausts at one stroke, therefore, all future possibilities of making decisions which could alter his orientation.

The second point of contact between the hypothesis of a final decision and a problem of theology is the doctrine of *salvation as personal fellowship with Jesus Christ.* In the theologian's mind two basic demands are ever present. On the one hand, he must accept that in principle salvation is possible for all, even for those who do not know God explicitly or cannot characterize him as God. On the other hand, he finds himself face to face with the unqualified requirement to see salvation as a personal relation with Jesus Christ and the express adoption of an attitude for or against him. The hypothesis of a final decision enables us to assure for all men a fully conscious and completely free stand as concerns the Saviour, individually and personally known as such.

The third meeting-point is the doctrine of the *universality of redemption*. Christ's redemptive act has created an all-embracing situation in the scheme of salvation. This is for all men, including the unbaptized and infants who have died without the use of their mental and spiritual faculties. Certain theologians suppose, however, that these infants had no possibility during their earthly pilgrimage of making any decision as concerns God and of so receiving at least the baptism of desire. But, without this sacramental incorporation into the body of Christ no salvation is possible, and so, since they are eager to avoid pronouncing any sentence of damnation on these poor creatures, they try to suggest that there is for them a kind of border-state—limbo (*limbus parvulorum*)—in which, though they are for ever separated from God, they do not have to suffer the torments of hell. But this, of course, is self-contradictory. To be separated from God for ever signifies nothing less than to suffer all the torments of hell, that is, to live in a state of alienation from God realized in all the fullness of its being. The hypothesis of a final decision is able to provide for this complex of questions a solution that is speculatively fully satisfying. It does so by depriving of its object the quite arbitrary assumption that there are human beings who during their earthly pilgrimage are not capable of making a decision for or against God.

In the fourth place, the hypothesis of a final decision permitted us to throw some new light on certain important *problems arising out of the doctrine of original sin*. In particular we examined the question of the double significance of human death in the scheme of salvation, in the hope of making it easier to find a solution. Death is not only the punishment, expression and manifestation of sin, it is at the same time a sign of a first, merciful loving-kindness of God for sinful man. Seen in the light of the final decision human death can be considered to be a genuine salvation-event. Through its very character of separation, death makes it possible for us to step out of the existential environment of original sin and by so doing to escape from all connexion or association with sin.

Our fifth confrontation took place in the *doctrine of the state of purification*. The hypothesis of a final decision brings us a step nearer a solution in the very involved theological question of the forgiveness of any imputability of venial guilt still present at the time of death. It also enables us to think of the whole state of purification as a cleansing encounter with Christ, as an essential dimension of the final decision. This facilitates a theological interiorization of the whole doctrine of purgatory.

In the sixth place the *christological basis* for the hypothesis of a final decision was made plain. First of all, the hypothesis of a final decision establishes us in a position from which we can answer with an immanent reason the grave theological question why Christ chose to save us by his death rather than in any other way. Christ's human reality, the instrumental cause of our redemption reaches the perfection of its instrumentality only in death, for—the hypothesis of a final decision suggests—nothing that is human comes to the fully complete positing of its reality until it does so in death. Further, on the basis of our hypothesis was discovered an interpretation of the reality that Christ's death represents. This sees the four events of Christ's passing over to his Father: death, descent, resurrection and ascension, as one single happening. In this way the hypothesis of a final decision enabled us to obtain a unifying vision of the basic process of salvation.

For these six confrontations we chose the most difficult and involved questions in theology in order to show that the hypothesis of a final decision is able to bring a new and greater clarity even to these problems. If we were to draw one final conclusion from our philosophical as well as our theological considerations, it would be this: *Death is a sacramental situation.* As the basic sacrament it is present and active in the inner structure of each individual sacrament, and these, in their turn, are signs of grace stretching forward to life's supreme encounter with Christ—in death.

NOTES

NOTES

[1] [p. vii] André Malraux, *La Condition humaine*. [Engl. *Man's Estate*, London & Harmondsworth, Methuen & Penguin, 1948 & pp. 1961; Part 7, Kobe.]

[2] [p. x] The work here presented is a much enlarged version of an article published under the title: "'Sacramentum Mortis'. Ein Versuch über den Sinn des Todes", in *Orientierung*, 23 (1959), pp. 61ff. and 75ff.

The most important publications dealing with the hypothesis of a final decision are given here at once. Others on the same subject will be noted in the course of the work.

R. W. Gleason, *The World to Come*, Sheed & Ward, 1958, pp. 43–77. The same essay appeared in a more expanded form under the title: "Toward a Theology of Death", in *Thought. Fordham University Quarterly*, 23 (1957), pp. 39–68.

P. Glorieux, "Endurcissement final et grâces dernières", in *Nouvelle Revue Théologique*, 59 (1932), pp. 865–92; more important still: "In Hora Mortis", in *Mélanges de Science religieuse*, 6 (1949), pp. 185–216.

Karl Rahner, *Zur Theologie des Todes*. [Engl. *On the Theology of Death* (Quaestiones Disputatae, 2), London, Burns & Oates; New York, Herder & Herder, [2]1965.] See also: *Das Leben der Toten* (Schriften zur Theologie, 4), Einsiedeln, Benziger, 1960, pp. 429–437.

M. F. Sciacca, *Morte ed Immortalità*, Milan, Marzorati, 1959.

Roger Troisfontaines, "La Mort, épreuve de l'amour, condition de la liberté", in *Cahiers Laënnec*, 7 (1946), pp. 6–21. This scholar has since developed his ideas in: *"Je ne meurs pas . . ."* [Engl. *I Do Not Die*, New York, Desclée, 1963.]

[3] [p. 2] In the course of our philosophical considerations it will become abundantly clear that the definition of death as "the separation of the soul from the body" gives a totally inadequate idea of what really happens in the process of death. Nevertheless, I am using this incomplete definition for the moment in order to bring out the diversity of the ways in which medicine and metaphysics consider the fact of death.

In this connexion, it may perhaps be useful if I give my own terms for distinguishing clearly one from another the various kinds of death already mentioned in the text:

(1) *Clinical death* denotes the act of dying in which the cessation of the essential bodily functions occurs. This in no way means that the "separation of the soul from the body" has already taken place.

(2) *Relative death* describes the state obtaining after the cessation of function has lasted for some length of time. The soul can no longer express itself through the body and, unless some quite extraordinary clinical operation—or a miracle—occurs, the body is incapable of being reanimated.

(3) *Absolute death* is the moment when "the soul leaves the body". Existence is released from the condition of temporariness and attains its definitive state of being. It is at this moment, which we can describe metaphysically but cannot determine physically, that the final decision is made.

Depending on the cause of death, the lapse of time needed for the process of death to pass through all these stages may be greater or smaller. A fixed time cannot be given since the moment of absolute death cannot be determined. Various clinical experiments indicate that the time required to pass from one state of dying to the next should be reckoned as long rather than short. Theological thought adds to this two considerations: (1) The biblical accounts of resuscitation (resuscitation is of its nature only a reanimation; the moment of absolute death, the entry into the final state of being, had not yet been reached by the particular "corpse" in question) speak of three or, in the case of Lazarus, of four days at most; (2) The lapse of time between the death of Christ on the cross and the resurrection (which two events might be seen as Christ's *clinical* and *absolute* death) indicates a similar reckoning.

R. Troisfontaines, *I Do Not Die*, pp. 137–8, also proposes a threefold division for the process of death, but his system differs slightly from mine.

[4] [p. 3] In his essay, "Some Points of Eschatology", in *Word and Redemption*, New York, Herder and Herder, 1965, pp. 147–175, Hans Urs von Balthasar very appositely describes the whole change of perspective that has occurred in eschatological theology, "the storm center of the theology of our times. It is the source of severe squalls that threaten all the theological fields, and makes them fruitful, beating down or revigorating their various growth". We refer the reader to this essay for a representative bibliography of recent theological writing.

[5] [p. 3] P. Glorieux's "Endurcissement final et grâces dernières" is a veritable milestone in the elaboration of the hypothesis of a final decision. St Thomas Aquinas was unable to finish his *Summa Theologiae*, so we do not know with certainty what was his final

theory of death. Glorieux set himself the task—which he accomplished in a masterly way—of collecting the indications scattered about in the various works of Aquinas and of establishing on this basis the main lines of the Thomist conception of death. He notes that in important passages St Thomas quotes a phrase of St John Damascene's: "*Hoc enim est hominibus mors quod est angelis casus*", establishing a parallel between death and the situation of the angels in their moment of decision. This made it obvious that this parallelism can reside only in the fact that in death man has to make an "angelic" decision. With the help of this knowledge Aquinas' scattered statements on death can be seen in a new perspective. The Angelic Doctor had already formed the concept of the hypothesis of a final decision. Therefore, it would appear that our "new" theological approach can be found in Aquinas. Glorieux's is a model of inspired research in this field of the history of theology.

[6] [p. 4] This is the argumentation of, for example, F. Sola in his *Sacrae Theologiae Summa*, Vol. 4 (Biblioteca de Autores cristianos), Madrid, 1956, p. 158. Similar arguments are used by R. Mengis in his articles in *Schweizerische Kirchenzeitung*, 127 (1959), pp. 433–4, 446–7, 636–8, 651–3, directed against the first draft of the present work.

[7] [p. 8] Martin Heidegger, *Sein und Zeit*. [Engl. *Being and Time*, London, S.C.M. Press; New York, Harper & Row, 1962, pp. 279–311.] In an essay entitled *Tod und Fortleben*, first published in 1911–12, later amplified (1913–14) and supplemented (1916), and now available in *Schriften aus dem Nachlass*, I: Zur Ethik und Erkenntnislehre, Berne, Francke, 2nd ed. 1957, pp. 9–64, Max Scheler developed a train of thought anticipating Heidegger's most important insights into the problem of death. According to Scheler, death is "present in every experience", the "*a priori* of every possible experience"; this means that we can work out the structure of death on the basis of the changing content of human consciousness (cf. pp. 18–26). M. F. Sciacca, *Morte ed Immortalità*, depends on Scheler in establishing his thesis of human death as a decision.

[8] [p. 9] Heidegger, op. cit., p. 288.

[9] [p. 9] "Quomodo medici quando inspexerint valetudinem, et mortiferam esse cognoverint, hoc pronuntiant: Moritur, inde non evadit. Ex quo nascitur homo, dicendum est: Non evadit." St Augustine, *Sermo* 97, 3; 3 (PL 38, 590).

[10] [p. 10] "Si ex illo quisque incipit mori, hoc est esse in morte, ex quo in illo agi coeperit ipsa mors, id est vitae detractio: . . . profecto, ex quo esse incipit in hoc corpore, in morte est." St Augustine, *De Civitate Dei*, 13, 10 (PL 41, 383; CCL 48, p. 392).

[11] [p. 11] E. Coreth provides an impressive historical and systematic presentation of the transcendental method in an article: "Metaphysik als Aufgabe", in *Aufgaben der Philosophie*, Innsbruck, Rauch, 1958, pp. 11–95, especially pp. 40–9.

[12] [p. 13] Maurice Blondel, *Exigences philosophiques du christianisme*, Paris, Presses Universitaires de France, 1950, pp. 277–8 & 288.

[13] [p. 14] St Augustine, *Confessions*, 4, 4; 7–9 (PL 32, 694–5; CSEL 33, pp. 68–70).

[14] [p. 16] Plato, *Symposium*, 204B.

[15] [p. 26] For a better understanding of the philosophy of action, see:

Maurice Blondel, *L'Action (1893)*. Essai critique de la vie et d'une science de la pratique, Paris, PUF, reprinted 1950.

H. Bouillard, *Blondel et le christianisme*, Paris, Editions du Seuil, 1961—an important book. See also: "L'Intention fondamentale de M. Blondel et la théologie", in *Recherches de Science religieuse*, 36 (1949), pp. 321–402.

A. Cartier, *Existence et vérité*. Philosophie blondélienne de l'Action et problématique existentielle, Paris, PUF, 1955.

Henry Duméry, *La Philosophie de l'Action*. Essai sur l'intellectualisme blondélien, Paris, Aubier, 1948.

P. Henrici, *Hegel und Blondel*, Pullach b. München, Berchmanskolleg, 1957.

An important aid for the study of Blondel is: A. Hayen, *Bibliographie blondélienne (1888-1951)*, Paris, Desclée De Brouwer, 1953.

My description of Blondel's *analyse de conscience* inevitably narrows down the reality denoted by the concept *action*. For Blondel *action* is the urgent, impulsive, emotive spiritual being of the person, though the word might, at first sight, give the false idea of an all too simple voluntarism. Blondel is not concerned with volition in the ordinary sense. Perhaps it is the Scholastic *appetitus naturalis*, found at the root of every single individual activity of the mind and producing it out of itself, that most nearly approximates to Blondel's concept of the will.

[16] [p. 28] It is astonishing to see how closely related are Ernst Bloch's analysis of hope and Blondel's exposition of the dynamism of mind. The Marxist Bloch also attempts to discover "the still unfound, the experienced not-yet-experience in every experience already made" (p. 368). Using a method—not unlike the transcendental—of attaining the conscious by way of the manifestations of human existence, from the modest daydreams of everyday life right through the whole gamut of outlandish utopias and fantasies that mankind has never ceased imagining in politics, science and art, not

to mention religion, he tries to find the kernel from which all these manifestations draw their life, content, orientation, meaning and dynamism: "Something that shines upon everyone's childhood, something none of us has ever yet been in, viz. home" (p. 1628). Cf. *Das Prinzip Hoffnung*, Frankfurt am Main, Suhrkamp, 1959. See also my article: "Begriffene Hoffnung", in *Orientierung*, 25 (1961), pp. 40–4.

[17] [p. 31] Joseph Maréchal, *Le Point de départ de la métaphysique*, Vols. 1–5 (Museum Lessianum), Paris, Alcan, 1922–6; cf. especially Cahier 5: Le Thomisme devant la philosophie critique. Maréchal died in 1944 in Louvain and could not terminate his work—Cahier 6 was to have dealt with contemporary theories of epistemology. His influence can be clearly traced in the Neoscholastic philosophy of our time and its many publications. Some are mentioned here:

E. Coreth, *Metaphysik*, Innsbruck, Tyrolia-Verlag, 1961. See also "Metaphysik als Aufgabe", mentioned above.

Joseph de Finance, *Être et agir dans la philosophie de saint Thomas*, Paris, Beauchesne, 1945.

Etienne Gilson, *L'Être et l'essence*, Paris, Vrin, 1948.

A. Hayen, *L'Intentionnel dans la philosophie de saint Thomas* (Museum Lessianum), Paris, Desclée De Brouwer, 1942; *La Communication de l'être d'après saint Thomas d'Aquin*, Vols. 1 & 2 (two more vols. to be published) (Museum Lessianum), Paris, Desclée De Brouwer, 1957–9.

B. F. J. Lonergan, *Insight. A Study of Human Understanding*, London, Longmans; New York, Philosophical Library, 1957.

J. B. Lotz, *Das Urteil und das Sein*, Pullach b. München, Berchmanskolleg, 1957.

A. Marc, *Psychologie réflexive*, Vols. 1 & 2 (Museum Lessianum), Paris, Desclée De Brouwer, 1949; *Dialectique de l'affirmation* (Museum Lessianum), ibid., 1952; *Dialectique de l'agir*, Paris, Vitte, 1954; *L'Être et l'esprit* (Museum Lessianum), Paris, Desclée De Brouwer, 1958.

Karl Rahner, *Geist in Welt*, Munich, Kösel, 2nd ed. 1957.

Gustav Siewerth, *Der Thomismus als Identitätssystem*, Frankfurt am Main, Schulte-Bulmke, 1939; "Die Apriorität der menschlichen Erkenntnis nach Thomas von Aquin", in *Symposion. Jahrbuch für Philosophie*, Vol. 1, Freiburg im Breisgau, Alber, pp. 89–167. See also: *Das Schicksal der Metaphysik. Von Thomas zu Heidegger* (Horizonte, 6), Einsiedeln, Johannes Verlag, 1959.

[18] [p. 36] Henri Bergson, *La Perception du changement*. Conférences faites à l'Université d'Oxford les 26 et 27 mai 1911 (Œuvres. Edition du Centenaire), Paris, PUF, 1959, pp. 1365–92.

19 [p. 42] The simplest approach to Marcel's ideas will be found in the comprehensive work of Troisfontaines, *De l'Existence à l'être. La Philosophie de Gabriel Marcel*, Vols. 1 & 2, Paris, Vrin, 1953. This book provides an impressive synthesis of Marcel's published and unpublished writings. We are given something like a "Marcelian System", a thing the philosopher himself had never dared to do. In his introductory *Lettre-Préface*, Gabriel Marcel writes: "En rédigeant le livre que j'aurais voulu écrire vous aurez fait ce qu'au fond j'aurais dû faire moi-même et vous m'aurez rendu personnellement un très grand service."

20 [p. 42] One representative of the innumerable attempts to come to grips with this problem should be named: Martin D'Arcy's *The Mind and Heart of Love*, London, Faber & Faber, 1946, and Fontana; New York Meridian, [2]1956. This book deserves notice for its great breadth of vision and the wide theological, philosophical and literary culture which are found concentrated in it.

21 [p. 42] Gabriel Marcel, *Présence et immortalité*, Paris, Flammarion, 1959.

22 [p. 48] 2 Cor. 4. 16.

23 [p. 48] St Augustine, *Enarrationes in Psalmos* 131, 1 (PL 37, 1716; CCL 40, p. 1911); *De Diversis Quaestionibus*, 49 (PL 40, 31); 53, 1 (PL 40, 34). See also: *De Civitate Dei*, 10, 14 (PL 41, 292; CCL 47, p. 288).

The existential state designated by Augustine under the biblical name "the outer man" (cf. 2 Cor. 4. 16) stands, as far as I can see, if we look on it as an attitude to life, at the very focal point of a whole series of similar attempts at conceptualization: *divertissement* (Pascal), *the aesthetic stage of life* (Kierkegaard), *das uneigentliche Dasein* (Heidegger), *Entäusserung* or *Selbstentfremdung* (Marx), *mauvaise foi* (Sartre).

Several aspects of the dialectic of the two curves of life as presented here had previously been pointed out by Troisfontaines in *I Do Not Die*, pp. 133–56.

24 [p. 49] Alexis Carrel, "Physiological Time", in *Science*, 74 (1931), pp. 618–21. Cf. also *Man the Unknown*, London, Hamish Hamilton, 1935, & Universe Books, 1961; Harper & Row, 1936, Chap. 5, § 2.

Pierre Lecomte du Noüy, *Le Temps de la vie*. [Engl. *Biological Time*, London, Methuen, 1936, Part 2, Chap. 6, pp. 79ff.]

The best conspectus of the whole problem will be found in P. Fraisse, *Psychologie du temps*, Paris, PUF, 1957.

The description here given of the individual phases and of the crises which separate them is much indebted to Romano Guardini's short, but substantial and thoughtful study in: *Die Lebensalter.*

Ihre ethische und pädagogische Bedeutung, Würzburg, Werkbund-Verlag, 5th ed. 1959.

[25] [p. 56] See the present author's "Das Märchen. Einführung ins geistige Leben", in *Orientierung*, 23 (1960), pp. 37ff.

[26] [p. 62] A first sketch of what follows here was first published under the title: "Das dichterische Wohnen", in *Orientierung*, 24 (1960), pp. 174ff.

[27] [p. 63] "Poetry is not, as so many people think, a question of feelings, but of experiences. For the sake of a single line one needs to see many cities, men and things, to know animals, to feel how birds fly, to have learnt the gesture with which the flowers open in the morning. One must be able to think back to paths in unknown regions, to unexpected meetings and partings one had seen coming long before they actually occurred, to childhood days still shrouded in mist, to parents one could not help hurting when they brought one some joy or other and one did not understand—it was a joy for someone else—, to children's sicknesses that begin so strangely with such deep and trying metamorphoses, to days in quiet, modest rooms, and mornings by the sea, to the sea itself, to seas, to nights on board ship rushing past high in the sky, flying with all the stars. And even to think back to all that is still not enough. One needs to have memories of many nights of love, none of them like any of its fellows, of the cries of women in labour, and then of how light and white they are as they lie there sleeping and shrinking back into shape after they have given birth. Then one must have stood by as men died, kept watch by the dead in a room with the window wide open and the short, sharp rustling noises. And it is not enough merely to have memories. One must be able to forget them if they are many, and have the great patience to wait until they come again, for the memories themselves are not yet the thing. Only when they become blood, sight and gesture in us, nameless and indistinguishable from ourself, only then may it happen that in a very special hour the first word of a line arises among them and comes forth." R. M. Rilke, *Die Aufzeichnungen des Malte Laurids Brigge*, Leipzig, Insel-Verlag, 1931, pp. 25–7. [Engl. *The Notebook of Malte Laurids Brigge*, London, 1930; New York, Norton, 1949. I have been unable to see this book, and the above version was made direct from the German.—*Translator*.]

[28] [p. 66] In his tale, *The Eyes of the Everlasting Brother*, Stefan Zweig has a passage that gives a vivid portrayal of what a philosopher can only express laboriously. He describes the state of mind of a man who, of his own free will, went down into the isolation of a dungeon-cell and there experienced the birth of a new world. It is a perfect symbol of what can occur in a poet's isolation. "On the second

day he was able to stand up and got to know his icy-cold quarters by going over everything carefully with his hands. He felt how, at each step he took, a world was growing anew, and on the third day his wounds were closed over and his senses and strength were returning. He sat still and only the drops falling from the wall marked the passing of time, dividing the great silence into many small times that grew quietly by day and by night, just as a life itself grows out of thousands of days into manhood and old age. No man's words disturbed him, darkness stood unblinking in his blood, but from within him memory in all its variety welled up gently, flowed together by little and little in a placid pool of vision mirroring the whole of his life. All the partial experiences he had ever had ran together now into one single one, and a cool limpidity unruffled by any slightest ripple held the purified image in the rhythmic pulsing of his heart. Never had his sense been so pure as in this feeling of motionless gazing into a mirrored world." Stefan Zweig, *Die Augen des ewigen Bruders*. Eine Legende, Insel-Bücherei, No. 349, pp. 31–2.

[29] [p. 68] For the origin of the philosophical key-word "kenosis", cf. Phil. 2. 5–7: "Have this mind among yourselves, which was in Christ Jesus, who, though he was in the form of God, did not count equality with God a thing to be grasped, but emptied (ἐκένωσεν) himself."

[30] [p. 69] Cf. pp. 42–7.

[31] [p. 73] See my article: "Kunstbetrachtung als Erziehung zum Absoluten", in *Orientierung*, 23 (1959), pp. 225ff., 241ff., 253ff.

[32] [p. 73] Points well worth considering in any analysis of the *a priori* relativity to death of human liberty are to be found in Gaston Fessard, *La Dialectique des Exercices spirituels de saint Ignace de Loyola*, Paris, Editions Montaigne, Aubier, 1956.

[33] [p. 74] Cf. p. 2.

[34] [p. 75] A good indication of the lie of the land in this whole complex of questions, together with strikingly chosen and skilfully arranged quotations will be found in G. Trapp, "'*Humanae animae competit uniri corpori*' (*S. Th.*, I, 51, 1 c). Überlegungen zu einer Philosophie des menschlichen Ausdrucks", in *Scholastik*, 27 (1952), pp. 382–99. A useful supplement to this is S. Pfürtner, "Seele und Beseeltes in philosophischer Sicht", in *Freiburger Zeitschrift für Philosophie und Theologie*, 3 (1956), pp. 45–51. We must, unfortunately, forgo any idea of listing the most important philosophical works on the subject of "substantial unity". Such an undertaking would swell these notes to a disproportionate size. Etienne Gilson, *L'Esprit de la philosophie médiévale* [Engl. *The Spirit of*

Mediaeval Philosophy, London & New York, Sheed & Ward, 1950, pp. 181–8], deserves a special mention because of its very pregnant and concise presentation of the facts.

[35] [p. 75] Thomas Aquinas, *Comm. in 4 Sent.*, D. 44, Qu. 1, Art. 2, Sol. 1.

[36] [p. 76] Cf. Thomas Aquinas, *Summa Theologiae*, I, 89, 1, Resp.; *Summa contra Gentiles*, II, 81; *Quaest. disp. de Anima*, 15.

[37] [p. 77] Cf. Thomas Aquinas, *S. contra Gent.*, IV, 90.

[38] [p. 78] For a definition of the original concept of the word "heart", see Karl Rahner, "Some Theses on the Theology of the Devotion", in J. Stierli, ed., *Heart of the Saviour*, London & Edinburgh, Nelson, 1959; New York, Herder and Herder, 1956, pp. 131–55. On p. 133 he writes: "'Heart' as a basic, original word for the whole man denotes that innermost centre of the human person which is at the origin of everything else in the human person, the centre in which the whole concrete 'nature of man as it expresses itself, develops and slips away, in soul, body and mind, . . . is gathered together, seized upon [and remains]. The centre in which the whole of his nature is, as it were, connected up and firmly fixed' (H. Conrad-Martius). The centre from which, therefore, in a manner that is all his own, a man determines his attitude to other persons and above all to God, whose concern is with the whole of a man and who, for that reason, in the course of his divine activity either gives his grace to this heart-centre of man or strikes it in judgement."

[39] [p. 78] Christ descended into this "heart of the earth" in his death: *ἐν τῇ καρδίᾳ τῆς γῆς*, Mat. 12. 40. Karl Rahner's views on this whole question can be studied in the English version of his essay on death: *On the Theology of Death.*

H. Conrad-Martius establishes a basic and inalterable assignation of the soul to its bodily concretion, in four points: (1) The soul effects its essential realization of itself by directing this realization into a physical body (the excarnative direction); (2) The soul extends into and throughout a body by commanding all its emotions and movements; (3) The sensitive soul needs the body for the revelation of its inner stirrings; (4) For its ontic concretion the mind is assigned a bodily place on which to set its mark; these last three are the modes of the incarnative direction. These views are the occasion of H. Conrad-Martius's assuming that the soul, even after its separation from its present (largely disintegrated) corporeity, retains an *ethereal body* which is already hidden in this present body. This ethereal corporeity is a *connecting link* between the grossly physical body which the soul can manage to permeate only imperfectly, and the resurrection body which, as the really proper and final medium for the realization and revelation of the soul, will be adapted to it in a very different way and in a more truly essential way than our present body. The important thing in this is that Frau Conrad-Martius accepts an absolute assignation of the soul for its very being to a state of corporeity occupied by it in actual fact. As a result, an absolute separation of the soul from the body, an absolutely bodiless soul, seem to her to be not only foreign to its nature but indeed a contradiction of it. On the whole subject see: H. Conrad-Martius, *Bios und Psyche*, Hamburg, Claassen & Goverts, 1949; *Die Geistseele des Menschen*, Munich, Kösel, 1960. A good summary is provided by W. Joergens, "Der Tod als die unwesensgemässe Trennung zwischen Leib und Seele bei Hedwig Conrad-Martius", in *Münchener Theologische Zeitschrift*, 11 (1960), pp. 106–22.

As far as the retention of corporeity is concerned, our interpretation of the process of death can go a great deal of the way with Frau Conrad-Martius's. Nevertheless, the acceptance of a pancosmic incarnation (relative excarnation) seems to me to correspond better to the cosmic relationships of the soul's assignation to a body than does the hypothesis of an ethereal corporeity. It is, however, by no means improbable that both interpretations have the same end in view.

[40] [p. 85] Denzinger 1796.

[41] [p. 89] This intervention of God in the series of secondary causes is one of the most questionable concepts of a world of ametaphysical thought. In metaphysics, on the contrary, God's mode of operation is called "transcendent causality". The operation of the transcendent cause cannot be inserted at a point in the chain-succession of secondary causes. God remains high above all the operations of causes occurring in this world, because he is not one of the secondary causes but the source that confers on them the force of their causality. He is the reason of the world, not a cause alongside other causes in the world. Seen metaphysically, God is the transcendent reason of all reality in its being and operation, that is, he is not a cause contained in this world, not a kind of demiurge whose activity takes place within the confines of the world, not a portion of reality as we encounter it, not a member in the world's series of causes. God's spatio-temporal causality in the world is reserved for his supernatural activity in the scheme of salvation.

Seen in a purely metaphysical way God is always the transcendent —in simple language, the other-worldly—foundation for all secondary causes and, therefore, the transcendent reason of all causality in the world. (By "transcendent reason" we mean the ground of all being, overriding and surpassing all the categories into which all we meet with in this world can be classified.) As the transcendent and transcendental reason of causality in its totality, God's operation is never present otherwise than through the intermediary of finite causes; except in the supernatural order, it must always be represented by a created cause.

In a cosmos of this kind all the "sums work out" invariably, even without God, because God is not one of the causes that go to make up the sum. He is not a factor in the world and its *fieri*; he is the primal reason of all the causalities we classify into categories.

A consistently thought-out Christian metaphysics, therefore, sees no difficulty in conceiving of everything that belongs to the normal content of the world in a way utterly and exclusively limited to this world. It sees the world as something which, in so far as it is of the order of secondary causes, depends on nothing but itself. Christian metaphysics even goes so far as to forbid our smuggling God into the closed chain of classifiable causes, or adding him to the world. In the explaining of created reality, therefore, we should start from the principle that God in the act of creation posits the creature in the possibility of its own self-realization and ordains for it all the necessary conditions for this. The same principle forbids our assuming that God procures or effects by means of a special intervention any result he can achieve through the immanent *fieri* of the creature itself. Any constant calling in of special interventions on God's part in the *fieri* of his creation appears in this view to be nothing but bad metaphysics and, in the long run, an untenable compromise.

These lines of thought can be pursued further in my article: "Evolution und Metaphysik", in *Orientierung*, 25 (1961), pp. 237ff. In this article the metaphysical concept of God's transcendent causality is applied to evolutionist cosmology, and more particularly to the creation of the soul immediately by God. The thoughts I developed there were occasioned partly by Karl Rahner's important philosophical and theological investigations into the problem of "hominization": "Theologische Anthropologie und moderne Entwicklungslehre", in the book: *Die evolutive Deutung der menschlichen Leiblichkeit*, Freiburg im Breisgau, Alber, 1960, pp. 180–210, especially pp. 190–203; and again: "Die Hominisation als theologische Frage", in P. Overhage & Karl Rahner, *Das Problem der Hominisation* (Quaestiones Disputatae, 12–13), Frieburg im Breisgau, Herder, 1961, pp. 13–90, especially pp. 43–84.

Similar ideas have recently been expressed by Gustav Siewerth, "Die Grenzen der Freiheit und die Verantwortung des Menschen", in the book: *Ida Friederike Görres. Festschrift zum 60. Geburtstag*, Zürich, Thomas-Verlag; Paderborn, Schöningh, 1961, pp. 161–2.

H. E. Hengstenberg represents a not dissimilar point of view in his book: *Sein und Ursprünglichkeit*, Munich, Pustet, 1958. For him God's transcendent causality becomes a "transcausal" mode of operation.

[42] [p. 89] Thomas Aquinas, *S. Th.*, Suppl., 69, 2, Resp.

[43] [p. 94] "*Hoc enim est hominibus mors quod est angelis casus*," John of Damascus, *De Fide Orthodoxa*, 2, 4 (PG 94, 877C). See also: Thomas Aquinas, *In 2 Sent.*, D. 7, Qu. 1, Art. 2; *In 4 Sent.*, D. 46, Qu. 1, Art. 3; *De Veritate*, 24, 10, Sed contra 4; *S. Th.*, I, 64, 2. [The English text gives a literal translation of the Damascene's statement as quoted—correctly—by St Thomas. The author's German translation gives the following in English: "Human death is a situation similar to the situation of the angels' decision."—*Translator.*]

[44] [p. 95] Cf. pp. 25ff.

[45] [p. 95] M. F. Sciacca, *Morte ed Immortalità*, develops a similar line of thought.

[46] [p. 96] Cf. Henri de Lubac, *Sur les Chemins de Dieu.* [Engl. *The Discovery of God*, London, Darton, Longman & Todd; New York, Kenedy, 1960, p. 156.]

D. Mollat also points out this double character of divine love, in his remarkable study on judgement, as one of the really essential Johannine themes. Cf. his article: "Jugement", in *Dictionnaire de la Bible, Supplément*, 4, col. 1383–4.

This point raises a new possibility of confrontation between a theological problem and the hypothesis of a final decision: the difficult and tragic question of the destruction of faith in the damned. If we take the case of damnation following on a mortal sin that was not a sin against faith, then faith really ought to continue in existence since it can only be reduced to nothingness by a sin opposed to it. How then does one explain that there is no more faith in hell? Does God himself destroy the faith of the damned by a personal intervention? Or is another sin that takes away faith committed after the act of damnation? The solution of this question would be a great deal simpler if we were to accept that the final decision involves the whole supernatural orientation of a man, including his faith. The final decision is either complete gift or complete rejection. Seen in this way, every act of damnation would be the consequence of a sin that is undoubtedly one against faith and, indeed, against the Holy Ghost. Cf. P. Glorieux, "In Hora Mortis", in *Mélanges de Science religieuse*, 6 (1949), pp. 207–8.

[47] [p. 99] Troisfontaines, *I Do Not Die*, cf. pp. 151–6

[48] [p. 100] Thomas Aquinas, *S. Th.*, II-II, 2, 7; *In 3 Sent.*, D. 25, Qu. 2, Art. 2; *De Veritate*, 14, 11.

[49] [p. 100] Thomas Aquinas, *S. Th.*, III, 68, 2.

[50] [p. 100] Thomas Aquinas, *In 3 Sent.*, D. 25, Qu. 2, Art. 1, Sol. 1, ad 1, ad 2; *De Veritate*, 14, 11, ad 1.

[51] [p. 104] In addition we may point out that St Thomas's theory of an immediate illumination of the human soul, reinterpreted as the attainment of perfect consciousness in death, would lose its character of a *deus ex machina*. It would no longer be an artificial, extraordinary and miraculous intervention of God in the human soul, but an event implanted in every man in virtue of the fact that his existence is created and formed for and in view of death, and, as such, valid in every human being. If a man, by the very fact of the spiritual dynamism of his nature, is, in every stirring of his existence *a priori* striving to come into union with God; if—as we accept—the same man is, in death, brought face to face with the totality of his spiritual dynamism, he needs no "special" illumination in death. At this moment the supernatural light that ever surrounds the human spirit mysteriously and without which man as a concrete historical essence is absolutely unthinkable, becomes a fact of integral consciousness. Man is brought face to face with God without any "special" illumination, by a simple conscious experience in death of the fact that a man's existence *is* illuminated.

Perhaps even, it would be easier to understand, in the hypothesis of a final decision, why St Thomas makes such explicit reference to the role of the angels in this respect. Karl Rahner noted that an angelology more deeply elaborated on the basis of a thoroughgoing biblical theology and sound metaphysics would demonstrate that a relationship with the world in its totality is an essential and permanent attribute of the angels. The planting in the basis of the world brought about in death would signify as well a planting in the sphere of the angels. Cf. Karl Rahner, *On the Theology of Death*, pp. 31–2.

[52] [p. 107] A good summary of the problems raised by the limbo hypothesis can be found in P. Gumpel, "Unbaptized Infants: May they be Saved?", in the *Downside Review*, 72 (1954), pp. 324–457; "Unbaptized Infants: A Further Report", ibid., 73 (1955), pp. 317–56.

L. Renwart gives us a very good orientation, the fruit of much reading, in "Le Baptême des enfants et les limbes", in *Nouvelle Revue Théologique*, 80 (1958), pp. 449–67, especially pp. 458–66.

Renwart examines in particular the question of the theological importance that we must attach to Pius XII's address of 29 October 1951. The pope declared: "In the present order there is no other means [apart from baptism in water] of communicating supernatural life to an infant that has not yet reached the use of reason." This papal pronouncement on the occasion of a congress of Italian midwives is frequently quoted against the hypothesis of a final decision. Renwart shows that the opinions of theologians vary enormously in their judgement as to the theological authority of this address. A central position is that of A. Minon, formulated as follows: "Le Pape Pie XII, se plaçant à un point de vue pratique . . . , ne prétendait certes pas exclure la solution large qu'il n'envisageait pas; mais il confirmait plutôt, sans l'imposer, la sentence la plus stricte." Cf. "Le Salut des enfants morts sans baptême", in *Revue ecclésiastique de Liège*, 38 (1951), p. 392. As far as speculative theology is concerned, therefore, the whole question remains open, even after this papal address. That is the conclusion reached by Renwart also.

[53] [p. 108] On the whole question see: Karl Rahner, "Eine Antwort", in *Orientierung*, 14 (1950), pp. 141–5. The same article in an expanded form appears as: "Über das Verhältnis von Natur und Gnade", in *Schriften zur Theologie*, 1, pp. 323–45. [Engl. "Concerning the Relationship between Nature and Grace", in *Theological Investigations*, I, London, 1961, pp. 297–317.] Still further precisions in "Über das Verhältnis des Naturgesetzes zur übernatürlichen Gnadenordnung", in *Orientierung*, 20 (1956), pp. 8–11. The whole matter can be studied in the well-informed article by L. Malvez, "La Gratuité du surnaturel", in *Nouvelle Revue Théologique*, 75 (1953), pp. 561–8, 673–99. Useful indications are also given by P. Fransen, "Pour une psychologie de la grâce divine", in *Lumen Vitae*, 12 (1957), pp. 209–40.

[54] [p. 109] These considerations bring us to a further question. Does the hypothesis of a final decision oblige us to assert that since baptized infants must make another decision in death, they can by their free decision in death bring about their own damnation? The possibility of self-damnation in the case of baptized infants dying in the state of baptismal grace would seem to be excluded by the *sensus fidelium*.

On this subject the following observation can be made. The hypothesis of a final decision reveals an important difference between the lot of the baptized infant and that of the unbaptized infant in death. It is not a matter of indifference if an infant dies with baptism, i.e. with its previous acceptance into the death of Christ and consequent gift of grace, or if it dies without baptism. In the first case it possesses the reality of grace, in the second it has merely the possibility of grace. It possesses the reality of grace since in baptism the child was accepted into the fellowship of Holy Church with infallible effect and with equally infallible effect became a subject of God's sanctifying lovingkindness. The fact that the child still has to endorse this lovingkindness by a free act in death makes no change in the finality of its present state of salvation. God's grace is able to direct the decision infallibly into the way of salvation while, at the same time, leaving the decision absolutely free. Expressed in Scholastic terminology our distinction would be as follows: *In sensu diviso* even infants who die in their baptismal grace can make their decision for God or against him; *in sensu composito (cum gratia baptismatis)* their decision, in actual fact, is made for God.

This is what the general conviction of the faithful emphasizes, viz. the fact that infants that die in the state of baptismal grace go to heaven. No less than that; but no more either. We have here also a justification for the obligation of conferring baptism: only baptized infants can make their final decision in a state of grace, i.e. in a situation of being, in which they are attuned from within to a choice for God and in which they are infallibly driven towards God by the inner dynamism of the divine life dwelling in them.

[55] [p. 110] The reproach might be made that in the hypothesis of a final decision infants would not be deciding their salvation as *viatores*. We insist once again: as seen in the hypothesis of a final decision death belongs to our state of pilgrimage. Moreover, the momentary nature of the final decision makes not the least difficulty in our considering the whole process as a decision of our human pilgrimage. This is indeed the way in which St Thomas represents the decision of the angels: "Ad secundum dicendum quod angelus meretur ut viator, non quasi distans a termino, sed ut in termino exsistens." *Quodl.*, 9, 8 ad 2. Note also that he describes as follows the sources of knowledge of the created spirit "in the moment of the soul's separation from the body" (*in sua ipsa separatione a corpore*): "Ex quibus collegi potest quod anima post mortem tribus modis intellegit: uno modo per species quas recepit a rebus dum erat in corpore [this source would not be available to infants who died before acquiring the use of their senses], alio modo per species *in sua ipsa separatione a corpore* sibi divinitus infusas, tertio modo videndo substantias separatas et in eis species rerum intuendo [these last two kinds of sources of knowledge can be taken to be available to infants, and this would allow of their coming to a clear mental vision]." *De Veritate*, 19, 1 corp., & ad 1.

[56] [p. 113] St Irenaeus, *Adversus Haereses*, 3, 23, 6 (PG7, 964 AB). For important elements in this whole conception of original sin I

am indebted to Troisfontaines. See, for example: *I Do Not Die*, pp. 189–244.

[57] [p. 113] Gen. 2. 17.

[58] [p. 113] Gen. 3. 19.

[59] [p. 114] Denzinger 101.

[60] [p. 115] Karl Rahner, *On the Theology of Death*, Chap. II, § 1, pp. 42–3. [I have very slightly modified the translation.—*Translator*.]

[61] [p. 117] In this connexion I should like to draw attention to a point of Aquinas's teaching that has been generally neglected. Even if Adam had not sinned, any subsequent personal sin committed by any one of his descendants would have become a real hereditary sin for all those human beings who descended from this one sinful individual. Cf. *De Malo*, Qu. 5, Art. 4, 8; and see further *In 2 Sent.*, D. 33, Qu. 1, Art. 1, 3.

[62] [p. 118] To anticipate any possible misunderstanding I should like to make clear the sense of the concepts "nature" and "person" as used in the whole of this section. As Karl Rahner says: "'Nature' (objective presence, *Vorhandenheit*) and 'person' (existence, *Existenz*) are, of course, understood here in the context of modern metaphysics and the philosophy of existence. Man is a 'person' in so far as he freely disposes of himself by his decision, possesses his own definitive reality in the act of making a free decision about himself. By 'nature' is meant all that in man which must be given prior to this disposal of himself, as its object and the condition of its possibility.... The pair of concepts mentioned above have their roots in scholastic tradition. For instance, when a distinction is made between *peccatum naturae* and *peccatum personae*, this same distinction lies in the background: original sin is a *peccatum* of 'nature' because it is found prior to the free decision of the individual subject as an element in the space within which (the 'situation') man is first called to make his own 'personal' decision, and with regard to which he must take up a position by comprehending this situation in this way or that." *Theological Investigations*, I, p. 362, n. 2.

[63] [p. 118] As concerns the question of original sin's being antecedent to any decision, St Thomas expresses himself in a most definite manner. The first act of reflective mental discernment, i.e. the first act of the awakened mind, seizes upon the wholeness of being and attains God in the wake of a spiritual intuition by setting in an essential affinity with God all that is. By means of his spiritual nature man, from his origin, lives and moves so fundamentally in the presence of God that the very first stirring of his growth to consciousness is capable of seizing on God as the efficient basis of all reality. According to Aquinas, this means that original sin cannot

penetrate into the domain of the personal. If his very first decision orients and orders a man to God, then grace lifts this man out of the state of original sin. If, on the other hand, his first decision directs him against God, the "simple" state of original sin becomes integrated, in this man, into an act of personal sin. Cf. *S. Th.*, I–II, 89, 6, and parallels.

[64] [p. 118] This rediscovery of the person could be demonstrated with the following representative names: Max Scheler (see particularly *Wesen und Formen der Sympathie* [Engl. *The Nature of Sympathy*, London, 1954]), Martin Heidegger (in this particular connexion, *Being and Time*, Part I, Chap. 4, § 26, "The Dasein-with of Others, and everyday Being-with", pp. 153–63, is especially important), Karl Jaspers, Gabriel Marcel, F. Ebner.

Among Christian philosophers should be mentioned Romano Guardini, T. Steinbüchel, D. von Hildebrand, A. Brunner, Hans Urs von Balthasar.

For the concept of "being-with", see W. Brugger, "Das Mitsein. Eine Erweiterung der scholastischen Kategorienlehre", in *Scholastik*, 31 (1956), pp. 370–83.

[65] [p. 118] Johann Gottlieb Fichte, *Grundlage des Naturrechts*, Vol. III of the *Werke*, p. 39.

[66] [p. 118] [This short sentence in such barbarous English seems so typical of the author's style and of the general difficulties of translating German philosophy and theology into English that we give it here in the original: "Das Dasein entsteht im Wesensraum des Mit- und Zusammenseins."]

[67] [p. 118] [The author distinguishes in what follows between two forms of one and the same adjective: *existentiell* and *existential*. In the English version of Heidegger's *Time and Being* by John Macquarrie and Edward Robinson, these two German words are taken over without change. I have not followed this example, for the simple reason that the normal German form *existentiell* should—and does elsewhere—correspond to the normal English form "existential". English has no adjectival ending -el, still less -ell, and it seems making confusion worse confounded to use the normal English -ial, in the sense of the specialized German *-ial*. Faced with this difficulty I had at first thought of "ex-sistential" for the special use, but finally, in the interests of aural as well as visual differenciation, have I created the word "existentiary", in the meaning which the author will shortly explain.—*Translator*.]

[68] [p. 119] "Die aus der freien Beziehungsstiftung entstammende mitmenschliche Ineinanderheit" (p. 129).

[69] [p. 121] A. Portmann, *Biologische Fragmente zu einer Lehre*

vom Menschen, Basle, Schwabe, 1944; see especially pp. 45, 50–1, 67, 69 & 81. The idea put forward here returns like a *leitmotiv* in a number of works by Professor Portmann. See, for example, *Naturforschung und Humanismus* (Basler Universitätsreden, 42–43), Basle, Verlag Helbing und Lichtenhahn, 1960, p. 41.

[70] [p. 122] Does not this idea of "birth in the bosom of the community" call for a further exegesis of the Augustinian and Tridentine definition: "*propagatione, non imitatione transfusum*"? Cf. Denzinger 790.

[71] [p. 123] N. Hartmann, *Das Problem des geistigen Seins*, Berlin, W. de Gruyter, 2nd ed. 1949.

[72] [p. 125] The mystery of the Immaculate Conception of Mary, viewed in this light, would consist in the fact that God himself broke up this ontological structure of existentiary being-with. The sinfulness that from outside crowded about Mary's existence never became the inner content of her existence. From the very beginning God himself was her "existentiary being-with" for Mary, her fundamental existential situation and the principle of her self-understanding.

[73] [p. 125] This example might conceivably give rise to a misunderstanding. Is not the equivalent suggestion being made that original sin only lays hold of a man at the moment of birth and, therefore, that it is not present before birth in the existence of the embryo? No, indeed. From the very first moment of the ovum's fertilization the whole being of a man is already in an existentiary way "being-with". The embryo's being-with, of course, has a largely anticipatory character, but this anticipation is so very real that, as the example in the text clearly shows, it exerts its influence on the biological evolution of the particular existence. Existentiary being-with is present in the embryo's existence, therefore, not only as a potentiality but as an ontological anticipation, realized in fact and constitutive of the living existence. Being-with belongs even before birth to the constitutive content of the structure of this existence as composed of body and soul; it determines the evolution of the existence in realized fact, and is, in addition, as its integral orientation, directed towards the conscious achievement of all that is thus constitutively anticipated. Existentiary being-with—and that means also, the state of original sin—belongs to the definition of the nature of man's prenatal mode of existence and can only be removed by a wholly exceptional intervention of God's grace—as in the case of Mary's Immaculate Conception.

[74] [p. 125] This state of grace for the moment, of course, remains antecedent to any personal decision, and later, when the child has

reached the age of free decision, will have to be ratified in a personal act, will have to be transformed into *existential* being-with.

[75] [p. 127] A penetrating elucidation of the concept of concupiscence which we have here only briefly described, together with a discussion of the theological problems involved, will be found in Karl Rahner, "Zum theologischen Begriff der Konkupiszenz", in *Schriften zur Theologie*, 1, pp. 377–414. [Engl. "The Theological Concept of Concupiscentia", in *Theological Investigations*, I, pp. 347–82.] Cf. also: J. B. Metz, *Christliche Anthropozentrik*, Munich, Kösel, 1962, pp. 86ff.

[76] [p. 128] Against the suggested interpretation of original sin on the lines of the hypothesis of a final decision, the following argument is sometimes raised, taking as its basis a text of the Council of Lyons (1274): "Illorum autem animas, qui in mortali peccato vel cum solo originali decedunt, mox in infernum descendere, poenis tamen disparibus puniendas" (Denzinger 464). This is held to proclaim that there are in fact men who on account of "simple" original sin are excluded from the vision of God.

This objection can be answered as follows: An overwhelming majority of theologians, even of those who do not look favourably on our explanation of original sin, is of the opinion that the intention—and, therefore, the dogmatic teaching—of the Council's declaration was to establish the fact that punishment follows immediately on death: "Les documents cités veulent surtout insister sur le caractère immédiat (*mox*) de la sanction après la mort. Ne leur demandons pas ce qu'ils ne veulent point nous dire", A. Gaudel in *Dictionnaire de la Théologie catholique*, 9/1, col. 766–7. It is obvious that the Council was not concerned to make a dogmatic decision on anything but that particular point. The enumeration by the Council of the different classes of men to whom this immediate punishment applies is simply the reflexion of a theological conception of the time. It represents neither the direct statement nor the concomitant teaching of the Church.

One might perhaps find a pointer to our interpretation of original sin in the *Sermo de Praedestinatione* of the deacon Florus († *c.* 860) contained in a text quoted in the second canon of the Third Council of Valence (855) to illustrate another thought (viz. God's foreknowledge of it does not mean that sin becomes a necessity): "Nec ex praeiudicio eius aliquem, sed ex merito propriae iniquitatis credimus condemnari. Nec ipsos malos ideo perire, quia boni esse non potuerunt; sed quia boni esse noluerunt, suoque vitio in massa damnationis vel merito originali vel etiam actuali permanserunt" (Denzinger 321; PL 119, 99B & 100A). This text seems to make damnation for original sin dependent on an appropriation of it through a personal act of the will, *suo vitio*.

[77] [p. 129] On the basis of the double role of human death in the scheme of salvation (determined by the loss of the *donum immortalitatis*), one might well endeavour to demonstrate a like twofold role in the loss of the other praeternatural gifts. In the text we have already shown that death as separation was rendered ontologically possible by concupiscence (determined by the loss of the *donum integritatis*), by man's incapacity as a person for achieving complete identity with his nature. Concupiscence can, therefore, be seen as the lasting presence of "death as separation" in the whole life of a man. This means that it (concupiscence), as a condition of the possibility of the death-process, shares in the latter's role in the scheme of salvation.

As for the state of existential ignorance (determined by the loss of the *donum scientiae*) and a liability to suffering (determined by the loss of the *donum impassibilitatis*), we can attach these to the ontological cleavage in existence occasioned by concupiscence. This state would then, through the intermediary of concupiscence, share in the double role attributable to death in the scheme of salvation.

To sum up: In order that death as separation may be possible, mankind must be placed in a state of concupiscence. This entails further, by an essential necessity of nature, an existential ignorance and a liability to suffering. In this way the twofold role of death in the scheme of salvation extends to the whole area of the state of ensnarement in which man finds himself as a result of the loss of the praeternatural gifts.

[78] [p. 131] Alexander of Hales, *Summa Theologiae*, P. 2, Art. 107, Membr. 10; P. 4, Qu. 15, Membr. 3. Cf. also Albert the Great, *In 4 Sent.*, D. 21, Art. 1.

[79] [p. 131] Bonaventure, *In 4 Sent.*, D. 21, P. 1, Art. 2, Qu. 1. In various metamorphoses the same view is represented in Peter Lombard, and later also in St Thomas, *In 4 Sent.*, D. 21, Qu. 1, Art. 3, Sol. 1, and Duns Scotus, *In 4 Sent.*, D. 21, Qu. 1, Art. 1.

[80] [p. 132] Thomas Aquinas, *De Malo*, Qu. 7, Art. 11. Cf. Suarez, *De Poenit.*, D. 11, Sect. 4, Nos. 13–18; and De Lugo, *De Poenit.*, Disp. 9, Sect. 2, Nos. 35–42.

[81] [p. 133] Cajetan, *In I Part. Summ. Theol.*, Qu. 63, Art. 5, in fine.

[82] [p. 134] Denzinger 983.

[83] [p. 134] In the collective work: *Le Mystère de la mort et sa célébration* (Lex Orandi, 12), Paris, Editions du Cerf, 1951, pp. 279–336.

[84] [p. 135] "Ipse [Deus] post istam vitam sit locus noster." *Enarrationes in Psalmos* 30, s 3; 8 (PL 36, 252; CCL 38, p. 218).

[85] [p. 135] Hans Urs von Balthasar, "Eschatologie", in *Fragen der Theologie heute*, pp. 407–8.

[86] [p. 137] Ex. 3. 6.

[87] [p. 137] 1 Kings 19. 13.

[88] [p. 137] Is. 6. 1–5.

[89] [p. 137] Cf. Dan. 7. 9–10; 8. 17, 18, 27.

[90] [p. 137] Cf. Ez. 3. 23–6.

[91] [p. 138] Mat. 17. 1–6.

[92] [p. 138] Apoc. 1. 12–17.

[93] [p. 139] According to the view of purgatory here proposed (albeit only tentatively), the purification process would be a happening it would be quite out of the question to measure in the days and years of the time we live on earth. It "would not last a definite time; it would be effected in a present not subject to the temporal extension of our duration" (E. Brisbois, "Durée du purgatoire et suffrages pour les défunts", in *Nouvelle Revue Théologique*, 81 (1959), pp. 838–45; see p. 844. Our note owes the basic structure of its thought to this very searching article).

On the other hand, our conception of purgatory must do justice to the Church's teaching on the value of prayers for the departed. Our prayers are offered up here on earth in a duration that is measured in days and years. It can even happen that they are made a very long time after the actual death. The question, therefore, arises whether they do not arrive "too late", if we are going to assume that purgatory is a process which is intensive and not extensive in time. Does this not deprive the devotion to the Holy Souls of all its real basis?

The immediate answer to this question is as follows: The devotion of the faithful, in fact, shows an astonishing capacity for not allowing itself to be unduly impressed by the problems of simultaneity. A very widespread practice in the devotion to the Sacred Heart which originated at Paray-le-Monial is the so-called Holy Hour. The faithful console with their sympathy the Saviour in his human agony in the Garden of Gethsemane or in general in his Passion. From a speculative point of view this pious exercise faces the theologian with much more complicated problems than the question of the petition in time for someone dead accomplishing his purification in a process that is not extended in time. So it scarcely seems likely that our proposed conception of purgatory would trouble the devotion of the faithful to the Holy Souls.

If we now consider the speculative aspect of the question, we find that the two kinds of duration, that of the departed and that of the living, are not attuned to each other. There exists between them no relation of reciprocal mensuration. They represent two fundamentally different systems of movement of being. A decree of Pope Alexander VII dated 1666 condemns a conception of purgatory built up on an interpretation given by Dominic Soto (1494–1560), according to which our prayers for the departed are supposed to lose their efficacy after ten years, since no one could remain "that long" in purgatory. The condemned proposition: "Annuum legatum pro anima relictum non durat plus quam per decem annos" (Denzinger 1143) betrays a wrong idea about the relation of the two kinds of duration. Our prayers can never arrive "too late", for the non-relation of the two kinds of duration puts any sort of "too-late" completely out of the question. It is true that we cannot form any imaginative representation of this aparallelism, but nowadays Einstein's theory of relativity has quite habituated us to the necessity of banishing imagination when treating of paradoxical data of this kind in logic or mathematics.

Again, on the other hand, a certain transposition into terms of time for a "human" understanding of the process of purification would seem to be of very great use. Our only possibility of grasping existentially the meaning of the different "intensities" of suffering in the state of purification is for us to project the vertical dimension of this purification on to the horizontal dimension of our time. In his day St Thomas Aquinas was already considering the possibility of conceiving the "duration" of purgatory not in terms of time and extension, but in degrees of intensity of the purifying pains. See *In 4 Sent.*, D. 47, Qu. 2, Art. 3, Quc. 2, ad 5.

On the whole question consult *DTC*, 13/1, col. 1289–90.

[94] [p. 139] Cf. pp. 4–8.

[95] [p. 140] See, for example, *S. Th.*, I, 45, 2 ad 3; III, 75, 7 ad 2; *De Veritate*, 28, Art. 9; *Quodl.*, 7, Qu. 4, Art. 9; *De Aeternitate Mundi adversus Murmurantes.*

[96] [p. 140] The Thomist views will be found in the very perspicacious article by P. Glorieux, "Fieri et Factum esse", in *Divus Thomas*, 41 (1938), pp. 254–78. Numerous texts, in the applications we mention, are there quoted *in extenso.*

[97] [p. 140] Such questions as: Was the first man created in grace? Were the angels created in grace? Has the angel merited his beatitude? Was Christ sanctified in the very first moment of his conception? Had Christ as man the use, from the first moment, of free self-determination? Could Christ, at the moment of his conception, gain merits? Had Christ at the first moment of his conception the full

vision of God?—See *S. Th.*, I, 95, 1, especially obi. 5 & ad 5; I, 62, 3 & 4; III, 34, 1. 2. 3. 4.

[98] [p. 142] Thomas Aquinas, *S. contra Gent.*, IV, 41, and cf. 36; *S. Th.*, III, 13, 2 corp.; III, 43, 2 corp.; *In 4 Sent.*, D. 5, Qu. 1, Art. 2, ad 6.

Since Aquinas this physical instrumental causality of Christ's human nature (*instrumentum divinitatis*) has been maintained by many theologians of weight, e.g. by the whole of the Thomist school (with the exception of Melchior Cano [1509–60]). We find opposing conceptions in the two great Franciscan theologians, Alexander of Hales and St Bonaventure, and also in Vázquez (1549–1604), Cano, and amongst more recent thinkers, Billot (1846–1931), Pesch, Galtier. On the whole controversy, see:

J. Backes, *Die Christologie des hl. Thomas von Aquin*, Paderborn, 1931.

T. Tschipke, *Die Menschheit Christi als Heilsorgan der Gottheit unter besonderer Berücksichtigung der Lehre des heiligen Thomas von Aquin*, Freiburg, 1940.

See also the controversial essay by F. Mitzka, "Das Wirken der Menschheit Christi zu unserem Heil nach dem hl. Thomas von Aquin", in *Zeitschrift für katholische Theologie*, 69 (1947), pp. 189–208, in which is defended the thesis that St Thomas was an opponent of the doctrine, spread abroad under cover of his name, of the physical instrumental causality of Christ's humanity in the work of our salvation. Mitzka has obviously been influenced by the unengaging interpretation put on St Thomas by Cardinal Billot. The whole controversy, moreover, is to be connected up with a different discussion, viz. the closer determination of sacramental instrumental causality. The views adopted in this latter debate are usually transferred to the role of Christ's humanity in the working of our salvation.

For the patristic basis of the physical instrumental causality of Christ one can consult:

Louis Boyer, *L'Incarnation et l'Eglise – Corps du Christ dans la théologie de saint Athanase* (Coll. Unam Sanctam, 11), Paris, Editions du Cerf, 1943.

A. Lieske, "Die Theologie der Christusmystik Gregors von Nyssa", in *Zeitschrift für katholische Theologie*, 70 (1948), pp. 49–93, 129–68, 315–40.

E. Scharl, "Der Rekapitulationsbegriff des hl. Irenäus und seine Anwendung auf die Körperwelt", in *Freiburger theologische Studien*, 60 (1941), pp. 6–31.

For a further examination of the basic Thomist concept of participation through contact (*participatio per contactum*), see Gustav

Söhngen, *Die Einheit der Theologie*, Munich, Zink, 1952, pp. 107–39.

Noteworthy ideas will be found in Cyrill von Korvin-Krasinski, *Mikrokosmos und Makrokosmos in religionsgeschichtlicher Sicht*, Düsseldorf, Patmos-Verlag, 1960, especially pp. 199–285.

H. Schillebeeckx, "Sakramente als Organe der Gottbegegnung", in *Fragen der Theologie heute*, pp. 379–401.

Idem, *Christus—Sakrament der Gottbegegnung*, Mainz, Matthias Grünewald-Verlag, 1960. [Engl. *Christ, the Sacrament of the Encounter with God*, London & New York, Sheed & Ward, 1963.]

A general résumé of the whole subject is given in *DTC*, 8/1, col. 1318–23.

[99] [p. 143] "Non autem perficit instrumentalem actionem, nisi exercendo actionem propriam." *S. Th.*, III, 62, 1 ad 2; 19, 1 ad 2.

[100] [p. 144] In this perspective one also understands better why Christ's life and death form a unity in the act of redemption. In death, on the one hand, the decisions of a lifetime are gathered together, and in the individual decisions of a lifetime, on the other hand, death is being rehearsed.

[101] [p. 145] St Cyril of Alexandria, *Twelve Anathematisms against Nestorius*. Cf. Denzinger 123.

[102] [p. 145] Idem, *In Ioannem*, 4, 2 (PG 73, 565D; 577BD); *Epist. 50 (44): Exegesis ad Valerianum* (PG 77, 261D – 264D); *Quod unus sit Christus* (PG 75, 1360).

Eusebius Caesar., *Demonstr. Evang.*, 4, 13 (PG 22, 24–8).

St John Damasc., *De Fide Orth.*, 3, 19 (PG 94, 1080AB).

[103] [p. 145] Thomas Aquinas, *In 4 Sent.*, D. 5, Qu. 1, Art. 2, ad 6.

[104] [p. 146] Mark 5. 24–34.

[105] [p. 146] In this connexion it should be noted that the Ignatian exercise of the "application of the senses" in its final development: the mystical activation of the "spiritual senses", already known to Origen, handed on by Augustine and systematized by Bonaventure, comes to the intuitive knowledge of Christ's reality as God and man by no other way than by a spiritual apprehension of his corporeity. See the revealing article by Joseph Maréchal, "Application des sens", in *Dictionnaire de Spiritualité*, 1, col. 810–28; and the article by Hugo Rahner, "Die 'Anwendung der Sinne' in der Betrachtungsweise des hl. Ignatius von Loyola", in *Zeitschrift für katholische Theologie*, 79 (1957), pp. 434–56.

[106] [p. 417] Cf. Thomas Aquinas, *S. Th.*, III, 48, 6 ad 2.

[107] [p. 148] Cf. pp. 77 ff.

[108] [p. 148] Mat. 12. 40.

[109] [p. 149] The *καταβασις εἰς τὰ κατώτερα τῆς γῆς* (Eph. 4. 9) is interpreted as a *descensus ad inferos* by Chrysostom (*c.* 347–407),

Theodoret (*c.* 393 – *c.* 458), Oecumenius (6th cent.), Tertullian (*c.* 160 – *c.* 220), Victorinus (*c.* 304), Ambrosiaster (*c.* 475), Jerome (*c.* 342–420), Pelagius (*c.* 400), Estius (1542–1613), Cornelius a Lapide (1567–1637), Bengel (1687–1752), Hofmann (1810–77), Klöpper, Bleek, Meyer (1800–73), Kähler (1835–1912), Westcott (1825–1901), Robinson (1858–1933), Huby, Scott, Odeberg, Benoit (in the *Bible de Jérusalem*), Büchsel (in the *Theologisches Wörterbuch zum Neuen Testament*, Vol. 3, p. 642: "He descended *under* the earth, not *on to* the earth." Therefore, "the descent means the entry by dying into the abode of the dead"), Bousset (1865–1920), Lundberg, etc. A number of ancient and modern exegetes, however, understand this *κατάβασις* as the descent of Jesus on earth in the sense of the incarnation. Cf. Heinrich Schlier, *Der Brief an die Epheser*, Düsseldorf, Patmos-Verlag, 1957, pp. 192–3.

110 [p. 149] Christ's invasion of Hades and deliverance of the dead remains, of course, one of the essential aspects of the Redeemer's victorious descent into the underworld. This aspect is summarized as follows by Michael Schmaus: "Christ revealed himself to those of the departed of all ages and all peoples who had died in a state of union with God and were in a state of sinlessness but whose access to the vision of God was still barred because before the death of the Son of God no one might enter into the Holy of Holies (Heb. 9. 8). He brought to them the message that the hour of liberation had struck. This was the same good news as the thief on the cross was permitted to hear before he breathed his last (Luke 23. 43)". *Katholische Dogmatik*, II/2, p. 363, Munich, Hueber, 1955.

111 [p. 149] As Logos Christ had, of course, always occupied this central position, but as man he had to win it in death. Only in death did Christ the God-Man become the Kyrios before whom "every knee should bow, in heaven and on earth and under the earth" (Phil. 2. 8–11; and cf. Eph. 1. 20–1).

112 [p. 150] Mat. 27. 51.

113 [p. 150] Josephus, *Bellum Iudaicum*, 5, 5, 4 (210–14); Philo, *De Vita Mosis*, 2, 17–18 (84–8); cf. also Thomas Aquinas, *S. Th.*, I–II, 102, 4 ad 4.

On the whole subject: A. Pelletier, "La Tradition synoptique du 'voile déchiré'", in *Recherches de Science religieuse*, 46 (1958), pp. 161–80.

114 [p. 151] Our exposition borrows essential matter from Karl Rahner's argumentation in *On the Theology of Death*, pp. 65–75.

What paths lead to our assimilation and grasp of the divine that is ever flowing into us from the cosmos? What are the dimensions of the re-enactment in our life of the results achieved by Christ in his death?

What would happen if we began to live reflectively all those experiences to which we normally react only dimly, as it were on the outskirts of our existence? How do we explain the indigence of our existence that obliges us always to pass by reality leaving it on one side, even though it lies in front of us and we have merely to stretch out our hands to take hold of it? I made an attempt to deal with these questions in my article: "Die Welt beginnt heute. Dimensionen unserer Weltinnewerdung", in *Orientierung*, 24 (1960), pp. 127ff., 142ff., 174ff., 181ff.

[115] [p. 152] Karl Rahner, *On the Theology of Death*, p. 72. [I have, however, not followed the English translation in the present quotation.—*Translator*.]

[116] [p. 153] Col. 2. 15; Phil. 2. 5–11; Eph. 1. 21; cf. also 1 Peter 3. 22.

[117] [p. 153] *ἀρχαί, κύριοι, κυριότητες, ἐξουσίαι, στοιχεῖα τοῦ κόσμου, κοσμοκράτορες, δυνάμεις*: Col. 1. 16; 2. 10; 2. 15; 1 Peter 3. 22; Eph. 1. 21; 3. 10; 6. 12; Jude 6; 1 Cor. 8. 5; 2 Peter 2. 10; Gal. 4. 3; Col. 2, 8; Apoc. 14. 10.

On the whole question, see, e.g.:

M. Brändle, *Kosmische Mächte: Kol 2, 8–20*, Enghien, 1954, MS.

Heinrich Schlier, *Mächte und Gewalten im Neuen Testament.* [Engl. *Principalities and Powers in the New Testament* (Quaestiones Disputatae, 3), Freiburg & London, Herder & Nelson—later, Burns & Oates, 1961.] Schlier summarizes his views in the article: "Gewalten und Mächte", in *Lexikon für Theologie und Kirche*, 4, col. 849–50. Further important literature is given in the review of Schlier's book by W. Pesch in *Theologische Revue*, 55 (1959), pp. 8–9.

Oscar Cullmann, *Christ and Time: the Primitive Christian Conception of History*, London, SCM Press, 1951, pp. 191ff. A résumé of this is: "Autorités", in *Vocabulaire biblique*, Neuchâtel & Paris, Delachaux et Niestlé, 1954, pp. 28–31.

[118] [p. 153] Jean Daniélou, *Essai sur le mystère de l'histoire.* [Engl. *The Lord of History. Reflections on the inner Meaning of History*, London, Longmans; New York, Regnery, 1958, p. 54.]

[119] [p. 154] "We are not contending against flesh and blood, but against the principalities, against the powers, against the world rulers of this present darkness" (Eph. 6. 12).

[120] [p. 155] Pierre Teilhard de Chardin set forth his christological spirituality primarily in his discussion of the spiritual life: *Le Milieu Divin. An Essay on the Interior Life*, London, Collins, 1960, and Fontana; New York, Harper and Row.

See on Teilhard's spirituality: G. T. Vass, "Teilhard de Chardins christologische Spiritualität", in *Dokumente*, 15 (1959), pp. 353–63;

and Ladislaus Boros, "Ein Versuch über die 'geistliche Lehre' Teilhard de Chardins", in *Der grosse Entschluss*, 15 (1960), pp. 254ff., 364ff., 398ff.

[121] [p. 157] The Pauline view of salvation is a decidedly "corporeal" one. It is a "growing together with Christ" (Rom. 6. 5; Eph. 4. 15), a "being a member of Christ" (1 Cor. 6. 15; 12. 27; Eph. 5. 30), a "putting on of the body of Christ" (1 Cor. 15. 49; 2 Cor. 5. 1–3; Col. 2. 11–15; 3. 9–15), a "changing of our lowly body to be like his glorious body" (Phil. 3. 21), a "participation in the body of Christ" (1 Cor. 10. 16), a "being filled with the fullness of his deity" (Col. 2. 9; cf. Eph. 1. 23). That is why Christ "had" to be crucified, "had" to die, be buried and rise again, in order that the mystical incorporation in Christ's real corporeity might be realized. Christ died in order to become risen body, a body, that is, that exists and is active in the sphere of being of openness to the world, and is, for that reason, capable of assuming all men into itself. If that is so, then our working out of our salvation consists in a "with", in a "becoming one with the basic, original process of redemption", this "becoming one" being, of course, understood as an ontological reality. The redeemed man must be crucified together with Christ (Rom. 6. 6; 8. 17), die with him (Rom. 6. 8), be buried with him (Rom. 6. 4; Col. 2. 12), rise with him (Col. 2. 12; 3. 1; Eph. 2. 6), be made alive together with him (Col. 2. 13; Eph. 2. 5), in order to be glorified with him (Rom. 8. 17; Eph. 2. 6). Thus the redeemed man puts on Christ ontologically and really (Rom. 13. 14; cf. Eph. 4. 24; Col. 3. 10), and this is what constitutes his sharing in the redemption.

This explains why recent exegetes interpret the expression "body of Christ" not figuratively, but literally: the personal body of Christ as it now is, a risen body, is the basis of our redemption. There is no such thing as a "double" body of Christ (a risen one and a mystical one). There is only the one. In the process of salvation, we do not become members of a "mystical body", we become in a "mystical and hidden manner" real, actual members of the risen body. On all this, see: P. Erbrich, "Mystischer und auferstandener Leib Christi", and "Christus stirbt, um auferstandener Leib zu werden", both in *Orientierung*, 23 (1959), pp. 193ff. and 204ff. A further bibliography will be found there.

[122] [p. 157] To the objection that between Christ's death and resurrection there is a real lapse of time, and that, therefore, the two processes are events separated from each other in time, we reply with the distinction we set out in the methodological part of our investigation—the distinction between clinical, relative and

absolute death, between which relatively long stretches of time can lie. There is, therefore, nothing against our saying that Christ *died on the cross,* while we still fix the *act of his death* later, at the same time as the act of his resurrection.

[123] [p. 158] John 12. 32; see also: 3. 13–14; 6. 62; 8. 28; 12. 33.

[124] [p. 158] Cf. Eph. 4. 10; 1 Tim. 3. 16; Heb. 4. 14; 6. 19–20; 1 Peter 3. 22; and further: Rom. 8. 34; Col. 3. 1–3; Eph. 1. 20; Heb. 1. 3 & 13; 8. 1; 10. 12; 12. 2; Acts 2. 33ff.; 5. 31; 7. 55; Apoc. 3. 21; 5. 6ff; 1 John 2. 1; 1 Peter 1. 21; 4. 13; 5. 1.

[125] [0. 159] Heb. 9. 24.

[126] [p. 159] Eph. 4. 10.

[127] [p. 159] The real account is in Acts 1. 1–11, with a brief mention in Luke 24. 51.

[128] [p. 160] M. Brändle, "Entmythologisierung der Himmelfahrt Christi?", in *Der grosse Entschluss,* 14 (1959), pp. 354–7.

The basic study was published by Pierre Benoit: "L'Ascension", in *Revue Biblique,* 56 (1949), pp. 161–203, and the same scholar has given a summary of the position in Benoit, "Himmelfahrt", in H. Haag, *Bibel-Lexikon,* Einsiedeln, Benziger, 1951, pp. 714–19. Further bibliography will be found there.

See also: R. Koch, "Die Verherrlichung Christi", in *Schweizerische Kirchenzeitung,* 127 (1959), pp. 493–6.

[129] [p. 160] Early Christian and patristic texts will be found in Benoit, "L'Ascension".

[130] [p. 160] Dom Odo Casel directed attention to this liturgical evolution in: "Art und Sinn der ältesten christlichen Osterfeier", in *Jahrbuch für Liturgiewissenschaft,* 14 (1938), pp. 1ff. It is worth noting that relying partly on the fact that the early Church celebrated Easter and Pentecost as a single feast lasting fifty days, and partly on the fact that for the Johannine point of view death, resurrection and the outpouring of the Holy Ghost represent but one single process, i.e. the exaltation of Christ, certain exegetes want to incorporate the event of Pentecost into the fourfold and single process of death, descent, resurrection and ascension. See, for example, C. S. Mann, "The N.T. and the Lord's Ascension", in *Church Quarterly Review,* 158 (1957), pp. 452–65. It is a fact that in a sermon attributed to St John Chrysostom, but obviously written by Hippolytus (cf. PG 59, 735–46), he "gave up the ghost" is explained as a breathing of the Holy Ghost into the whole world.

[131] [p. 161] In this connexion we should ask the further question whether Christian death, since fundamentally it consists in the reenactment of Christ's death-process, does not also comprise in an indissoluble unity all the four elements, including the corporal

resurrection. That the forces of the world to come have already taken hold of our world, is made clear by the dogma of the corporal assumption of Mary into heaven. In the case of Mary's assumption mention is made of a privilege of the Blessed Virgin, inasmuch as, by reason of her unique position in the scheme of salvation, she had a special right to this assumption. But is it also a privilege in the sense that it was conferred on Mary alone? Troisfontaines answers in the negative: "Is the Blessed Virgin really the only one to share with Christ in the resurrection? It is impossible for us to affirm this. The saints who, in their lifetime, have overcome sin and spiritualized their body will certainly have a less intense sensation of being wrenched away in the parting of death, than we shall. There is no reason why we should not think that Christ lets them share in the total victory even sooner" (cf. *I Do Not Die*, pp. 293–4). Troisfontaines here quotes Mat. 27. 52–3: "The tombs also were opened, and many bodies of the saints who had fallen asleep were raised, and coming out of the tombs after his resurrection they went into the holy city and appeared to many."

The eschatological interpretation of this text (i.e. in the sense that the consummation of the last days has already begun) is now, in the light of the most recent research into the history of biblical exegesis, absolutely certain. Karl Rahner remarks on this passage: "It would not be in accordance with the undoubted meaning of Scripture if one were to try and get rid of this witness in Matthew as a very 'mythological' interpolation. It would be just as mistaken to attempt to explain away the eschatological meaning of this text by means of artificial sophistries, arguing, for instance, that it is nothing but a temporary resurrection, or that the bodies are only 'spiritual bodies'. As a matter of fact, by far the greater number of the Fathers and theologians right up to our own day have always maintained the eschatological interpretation of this text, the only one that is exegetically possible." Cf. "Zum Sinn des neuen Dogmas", in *Schweizer Rundschau*, 50 (1951), p. 590.

On the history of the exegesis of Mat. 27. 52–3, see the outstanding study of H. Zeller, "Corpora Sanctorum", in *Zeitschrift für katholische Theologie*, 71 (1949), pp. 384–465. Theologically, therefore, there is not only a possibility, there is also actual certitude that events we usually call the "last things" have already begun. With Christ's death and resurrection the whole of history has already been overtaken. The end of the world has already begun, although history, overtaken in the redemption, did receive some scope again and the harvesting of salvation did recover its historical dimension of extension in time.

If we assume that Christian death, i.e. the final decision in favour of the Redeemer, is also the Christian's resurrection and ascension, this would mean a considerable enrichment for the hypothesis of a final decision, an enrichment altogether in the logic of our basic thesis. Our philosophical considerations already contained some hint of this. There we discovered the following points: In every spiritual act man aims at reshaping in a personal way what he finds present in himself (and as himself) by nature. This, however, is possible only on two conditions: (1) if he can lay aside his body and his relationship with the "given" world about him and connected with him; and (2) if he himself can be the origin of a new incarnation.

In this way, even a purely philosophical perspective would show that death is the place of total liberty, i.e. the place in which the individual existence refashions its outward appearance, its own bodily form. The eschatological interpretation of Mat. 27. 52–3, and the conception this announces of the end of the world as having already begun, prove that this perspective is not altogether foreign to our theology.

It remains to emphasize one final point in these considerations: the nature of the resurrection as a properly eschatological event would keep all its significance in the proposed interpretation of Christian death. (1) It would bring about the open manifestation of what has already happened in the hidden secrecy of eternal life. (2) Since the transformation into glory of the cosmos will not be made manifest until the end of time, and since the risen body of the saint needs the transformed cosmos as its existential environment, the coming of the end of the world would bring with it a last consummation of the resurrection that has already occurred in death. Therefore, the category "betwixt-and-between", basic to the scheme of salvation, is applicable to the immediate resurrection in death which we are assuming here as an hypothesis. This basic category we call "betwixt-and-between"—the thing has already happened but is not yet fully completed—is also used in other eschatological propositions. The statements of revelation about the end of the world, e.g.: ". . . with the angel's call, and with the sound of the trumpet of God. And the dead in Christ will rise first" (1 Thess. 4. 16; cf. 1 Cor. 15. 23; Denzinger 40, 530) lose nothing whatever of their value. They are merely put into the context of other eschatological statements of Scripture and explained in that context.

[132] [p. 164] Our real task here was not so much to prove the sacramentality of death (understood, of course, only in an analogous sense). We were more concerned with working out its relation

with the seven sacraments. There were two possible ways of doing this.

(1) Starting from a "non-punctual" consideration of the sacraments we could show in what way a sacrament was existentially built into the Christian life, that is, how it works itself out in no other way than in a "being for death" and, therefore, reaches its full flowering only in death. An example would be to show how baptism is the beginning, made sacramentally visible, of the death that represents the climax of the personal appropriation of salvation, and then to show how as a result of this it is operative through the whole course of the baptized man's life, receiving its complete reality only in death. The same situation could be demonstrated in the other sacraments too, more particularly in the central sacrament of the Christian Church, the Eucharist.

(2) It would be possible to show, by a logical development of the structures of our "sacramental metaphysics", that the individual sacraments for their part are signs of the final encounter with Christ which is ours, through a sign, in death. By this approach the metaphysical position of death as the basic sacrament in the individual sacraments could be more precisely determined. In this perspective the sacraments would be seen to be so many acts stretching forward, as signs filled with grace, towards the situation of death in which the complete being-with with Christ and, as a result, the perfect communion with all men who are striving to reach Christ, are offered to each one of us. Thus, in the visible shape of the individual sacraments, that which is offered us in death, would also be attaining a state of visibility.

If we are to remain within the proper field of our present investigation, we cannot offer the reader more than these brief indications.